CROSS-CURRENTS IN THE

PERSONALITY OF

MARTIN LUTHER

CROSS-CURRENTS IN THE PERSONALITY OF MARTIN LUTHER

A Study in the
Psychology of Religious Genius

By

VERGILIUS FERM, Ph. D.

The Christopher Publishing House
North Quincy, Massachusetts

Copyright © 1972
BY VERGILIUS FERM
Library of Congress Catalog Card Number 75-189362
ISBN: 1-8158-0277-3

PRINTED IN
THE UNITED STATES OF AMERICA

To
The Memory Of
Professor Edwin Diller Starbuck

OTHER BOOKS BY VERGILIUS FERM

The Crisis in American Lutheran Theology, 1927

What Is Lutheranism? (ed.), 1930

Contemporary American Theology, Vol. I (ed.)., 1932

Contemporary American Theology, Vol. II (ed.), 1933

First Adventures in Philosophy, 1936

First Chapters in Religious Philosophy, 1937

Religion in Transition (ed.), 1937

An Encyclopedia of Religion (ed.), 1945

Religion in the Twentieth Century (ed.), 1948

What Can We Believe? 1948

Forgotten Religions, Including Some Living Primitive Religions (ed.), 1950

A History of Philosophical Systems (ed.), 1950

A Protestant Dictionary, 1951

The American Church of the Protestant Heritage, (ed.), 1953

Jonathan Edwards, Puritan Sage (ed.), 1953

The Protestant Credo (ed.), 1953

Their Day Was Yesterday (A Novel), 1954

A Dictionary of Pastoral Psychology, 1955

In the Last Analysis, 1956

An Encyclopedia of Morals (ed.), 1956

A Pictorial History of Protestantism, 1957

A Brief Dictionary of American Superstitions, 1959

Classics of Protestantism (ed.), 1959

Inside Ivy Walls, 1964

Toward an Expansive Christian Theology, 1964

Basic Philosophy for Beginners, 1969

Memoirs of a College Professor, 1971

So . . . You're Going to College, 1972

TABLE OF CONTENTS

INTRODUCTION—I

There were three of us who sat around a large table in the small library-room upstairs in one of the main class-room buildings on the University of Iowa campus. The time: the late teens of this century. The room was dingy, stuffy, unattractive. It was a place reserved for graduate students in philosophy. Each of us had books piled around our places at the table which gave us some sort of privacy. The day of the library carousel—private booths—had not yet arrived. We respected each other's desire for silence. Hardly ever did we speak to one another.

The three were: Rachel Knight, Herman Hausheer and I. Each one was engaged in a piece of research related in general but altogether different in topics. Miss Knight had George Fox's publications and related material piled high around her place of concentration; Hausheer had Augustine's works and supporting material; and I had amassed a wall of volumes relating to Martin Luther. We had a common base of interest. We were graduate students doing work toward degrees (and in Miss Knight's case: publication) under the same professor and this professor had seemingly chosen us as his special students to work out a theory or point of view which he himself had become excited over: in the area of the psychology of a religious genius, or more specifically, what made some conspicuous religious leaders tick? Already there had appeared a series of articles by the professor in a major encyclopedia and other journals in which the germ of his ideas on the subject had been expounded and he was anxious for his researchers to develop the seminal idea as it (perhaps) got expressed in three historic religious personalities.

I had no idea when I came to Iowa University Graduate School in the fall of 1919 that sooner or later I would meet up with Professor Edwin Diller Starbuck. And, of course, I had no idea of his academic eminence. Already, William James of Harvard had spotted him. In James' famous *Varieties of Religious Experience,* published at the turn of the century, Starbuck's researches in adolescent psychology had received a conspicuous place. There seemed to be a correlation of psycho-physiological adolescence with both the fact and the type and the degree of what had long been called "conversion" and James played this up (on this theme) and gave Starbuck full credit for the use of statistical studies which appeared in Starbuck's earlier book entitled *The Psychology of Religion* (a pioneer study in the field).

When we landed at Iowa as graduate students we were, by good luck, sparked by his enthusiasm and directed to the study of why some people (aside from mere historical accidents) become psychologically notable and move in on their day and cut through the crust of traditions and make their mark.

Miss Knight's thesis on George Fox had already been finished when I came upon the scene. I was quite unaware that she had already earned her doctorate and was now working the material into a book. Much later I came across a notice of it. The title: *The Founder of Quakerism* (A Psychological Study of the Mysticism of George Fox) published in 1922 in England. Her thesis not only followed the significance of a manifold of conflicting traits in the personality of Fox but it followed somewhat closely Starbuck's suggestion (in his published articles) that "the intimate senses"—perhaps ultra-microscopic sense organs operating internally in the physical organism—stimulated awareness in some persons more powerfully than in others, thus setting them off from the run-of-the-mill of humanity. May there not be such end-organs on the intestines, receptors giving those so endowed certain awarenesses, appreciations, frustrations, variances, restlessness, insights, even "mystic" insight? Her book followed through with such an hypothesis, digging into the *Journals* (of Fox) and finding hints of his more or less strange powers of awareness—and thus explaining the roots of his genius. The religious side of a person's interest is thus perhaps exercised in ways strange and unusual (about which Fox wrote) and his sense-perceptions stimulated him to new slants on life's experiences.

I recall Miss Knight's physical person. She carried enormous weight and she seemed not only visibly suffering under it by a continual puffing but she sweated enormously. I recall one idiosyncracy: she wrote with a pencil the size of a healthy match and it seemed always hid in her hand, her chubby fingers laboring to control it. When I heard of her untimely death (it occurred in 1921 before the publication of her book) I was not too surprised. Nor was I surprised to see that her book (edited by a British scholar) carried her dedication to our beloved professor, scholar and friend, Edwin Diller Starbuck.

Hausheer was a fine scholar and I recall having seen his doctor's thesis, a huge tome on the criss-crossings of Augustine's own psychic make-up. Hausheer and I corresponded through the years, he responding to my request for articles on philosophers, theologians and psychologists (mostly foreign) for the work I was editing called *An Encyclopedia of Religion* (1945). His academic career came late in life. I doubt that his main *opus* ever saw the light of publication—other than perhaps under separate articles.

Circumstances—quite beyond my prediction —came into my life while I was in the midst of the study of Luther's personality along the lines outlined above and rudely jerked me away from the routine of study I had been following at Iowa under Professor Starbuck. Reviewing such events does not belong here and I have written them down in an autobiography recently published, entitled *Memoirs of a College Professor* (1971), in which I relate my brief encounter with the fine scholars at Iowa University at a period rather early in my graduate academic life. It was the writing of this chapter of my experiences that brought out from my subconscious mind a memory of some unfinished work that I had thought to be doing on the third character of this study of a trinity of religious geniuses. My bout with Luther suggested a personality beautifully fit for the Starbuck hypothesis that a religious genius is a heterogeneous personality who operates in the area of religion. The field of operation is much more secondary than the intrinsic make-up of the personality. It is quite probably accidental what fields a person pursues as a specialization. To whatever field he happens upon and to which he applies himself, his personality gives to it an imprint; if his is a complicated personality, then, other things being equal, he should be rich in insights and awareness and make for him a mark quite set apart from the general run-of-the-mill humanity.

I wrapped up my study of Luther and called it "Cross-Currents in the Personality of Martin Luther—A Study of Religious Genius." I changed academic environments in the very middle of my studies by a twist of fate. And I registered myself as a graduate student at Yale hoping that in my first year there I might find the work already begun acceptable for academic recognition. Thus, in due time and after meeting certain of Yale's Graduate School requirements for an academic degree, my study of Luther was concluded. In 1923 the Yale faculty recommended me for the Master's Degree with the presentation of this thesis on Luther.

During the first year of course-study there, I registered for Roland Bainton's course on the Protestant Reformation—a seminar of some six or eight students. Professor Bainton was then in his budding years as a Reformation scholar and working upon what turned out later to be a major book on Martin Luther. Little did I realize then that my good fortune had brought me to a specialist not only on the period of the Protestant Reformation but to someone especially interested in the peculiarities and even the rough sides of the personalities involved in that general period. I got little from him of the current feuds going on among the psychologists but I learned a great deal of the times of the sixteenth century of European history.

I would be remiss if not ungrateful if I did not mention Dr. Luther A. Weigle who took me under his wing in those earlier days. Dr. Weigle who (while I was there) became Dean of the Yale Divinity School was then in his professional prime and offered a course in the psychology of religion—perhaps the most popular lecturer of the Divinity faculty at the time. It was another priming of the pump for me to be introduced by him to the many current names and theories in non-behavioristic psychology and it was he who gave generously of his time to guide me in the organization of my Luther material—the subject of this volume.

It was my hot ambition after the psychological study of Luther to follow through on the great Reformer's "systematic" theology. I was ready to pour ammunition into the follow-up: a man like Luther could never be systematic! No wonder he loved the Apostle Paul and Augustine—personalities like himself of contradictions and quite unsystematic in their theologies. For Lutherans to quote Luther indiscriminately—which they did all over the place—was at many spots to unquote him. I could see in the immediate future a potentially good doctor's dissertation. And I asked that I might follow through with it.

To my chagrin, I was warned that such a study as I had proposed would meet with a road-block by the psychology department. How could Starbuck's thesis possibly buck the coming onslaught of the Behaviorists, hypnotized by John B. Watson who at this time was a campus lecturer at Yale (not to mention his sweep of all the important academic psychology departments in the U.S.A.). Watson's pale blue

hard-cover book on Behaviorism was already
at Iowa University a kind of Bible to be tho-
roughly known by any graduate student in
psychology. I knew that my path had an almost
insuperable road-block and I wisely agreed,
although reluctantly, to turn my attention to
another field of enquiry if I were to attain the
doctorate and live with my own academic conscience. (It is quite understandable now why my
Luther study finally ended up in my attic.)

Behaviorism at the time was radical: the
magic S-R bond (Stimulus-Response). It brought
an abrupt end to my interest in psychology as
a major field of specialty. I wanted something
more than undisguised or disguised biology or
physiology (important as these disciplines are).

There were other currents in the psychological field available: such as the then post-War
School of Dynamic Psychologists in England
(T. W. Pym, C. E. Hudson, R. S. Moxon, J. A. Had-
field, William Brown, R. H. Thouless and others)
who were very attractive. This and the developing neo-Freudian school of psychology looked
promising to me and did not mean a parting of
the way altogether from philosophy and theology and religion—at least for a graduate student
in the years of the early twenties.

So, the frustration happily turned me on to
new channels of interest and to my life-long
work in philosophy, theology, and comparative
religion along with social psychology.

The present book was developed some fifty years ago. I found a copy of the typescript in my attic (as I have already related) while writing my *Memoirs*. The thesis still sounds valid to me even though the literature of psychology (as in any other field of enquiry) has undergone many changes by new studies. The facts, however, are there: here was a complicated man with a striking personality. Many inductions could be made in "explaining" him. Any one may be correct or incorrect. This is the manner of all scientific enquiry (facts lend themselves to many theories). Professor Starbuck's thesis may still be suggestive even though hundreds of psychologists have moved into other pastures. I have no yen to follow other interpretations—that is, later books. But publishing this one—as old as 1923 when it was completed—does not render the induction then made necessarily invalid. It is the same person who is studied. The web of history remains constant, locked in the channels of specific time and space. Our theories change and often, indeed, render new insights. But the facts stubbornly remain.

Professor Bainton has agreed to allow me to publish his dated estimate of my thesis. He was a member of the committee giving approval of it at the time it was examined. He agrees with me now that the whole thing should be updated— even his own estimate of it at the time. (To update the bibliography—it seems to me—would be only a case of academic pedantry and for the purposes of this book quite unnecessary.)

I toss off this volume (at its perhaps adolescent age) as a kind of labor of love which occupied my mind seriously and under the inspiration of a great student of religous psychology whom I respected and who, in his day, was a pioneer in the field along with George A. Coe, E. S. Ames, G. Stanley Hall, J. H. Leuba, J. B. Pratt, G. M. Stratton and many other stalwarts of their day including the earlier speculative psychologist William James.

Is there not room on the book-shelves for another look at the psychology of personalities apart from one particular psychological school or segmented scientific approach?

At least, there is such a thing as philosophical psychology with the freedom to speculate upon data without being tied to stricter empirical psychological rules of the game (such as S-R or organismic functional response or some such other). I, for one, think that there is, at our date of time, a re-awakening among the psychologists themselves who, in their commitment to their strictly scientific rules, realize that they have lost a large area of their subject: areas involving the philosophical, speculative, and the broader scan of the psyche —what was once called philosophical psychology—the open field of the philosopher who is

willing to make mistakes for the prize of freedom and in the hope of some deeper insight
into the nature of human psychology.

Late Summer, 1970   *Vergilius Ferm*
Mercer Lake,
Mercer, Wisconsin

INTRODUCTION—II

Cross-Currents in the Personality of Martin Luther—A Study in the Psychology of Religious Genius

Vergilius Ferm.
Approved, May 22, 1923.
Opinion. Copy for Mr. Ferm.
Mr. Ferm has read widely and has collected a lot of valuable material. But he has not delved in quite the right quarter. Biographies by Roman Catholics like those of Janssen and more especially Grisar make a specialty of discrediting Luther on the ground of psychological abnormality. If these works had been read it would have been necessary to add a contrast between coarseness and delicacy.

In the section on cruelty I can find no use of the famous treatise "Against the Thieving and Murdering Band of Peasants."

The chronology should be more carefully considered. Mr. Ferm thinks that these cross-currents are to be found in Luther in equal strength at the same time. I rather doubt it in some cases. His melancholy was deepest in the early days when he had not arrived at justification by faith, and again at the end when he had unloosed the whirlwind and could no longer control it. His critical spirit was a matter of growth. I wonder whether the periods of self-exaltation do not correspond to times of conflict and the self-abnegation or depreciation with the depression which frequently followed.

A more careful arrangement and analysis of the material might have eliminated some contrasts. The condemnation of Aristotle and the papists does not necessarily involve any self-exaltation. Aristotle is disparaged in contrast with other philosophers and the papists in comparison with the gospel. Further self-exaltation is made to include confidence in his cause, which is easily consonant with self disparagement. No clear study is made of the amount of self-exaltation involved in the prophetic consciousness. Does Luther exalt himself because he thinks that God speaks through him? The standard of comparison is not always the same. It will not do to compare Luther's estimate of himself in comparison with his fellows and his estimate of himself in comparison with God.

Cruelty is made to cover invective as well as ruthlessness in action. Greater analysis would help here too. To whom is he cruel or kind? Men are often cruel to those without their own group and kind to those within. Again what is the principle of his cruelty? It is very common for men to crush their natural kindliness in the interests of a principle. Calvin said, "There can be no considerations of humanity when the glory of God is concerned." Cromwell said,

"Love your enemies as they are your enemies and hate them as they are God's enemies." This is the distinction which is often made between private and public wars. Again cruelty is often justified as ultimate kindness. The burning of heretics was defended in just that way. All these distinctions should be examined in Luther's case.

Humor in the sense of animal prankishness is easily associated with melancholy in the sense of a pessimistic view of life. The contrast would be remarkable if it applied not so much to mood as to views of life, if optimism and pessimism really alternated.

It is doubtful whether Luther can be called critical in a speculative sense at all. He had an immediate religious problem of getting right with God. That problem was solved through justification by faith. This solution was not in accord with the penitential system of the church, so the system had to go. The pope did not recognize this rejection so the pope had to go. But Luther rejected only that which imperilled his major premise.

The quotations on the practical side of Luther cover a wide range without any classification.

Finally what is the Christ experience? Just how does it synthesize cruelty and kindliness, criticism and superstition, etc.?

Again why are some of these contrasts introduced in the study of a religious genius? To be sure they existed in Luther and he was a religious genius, but some of them existed equally in men who were nothing of the sort. The conflict between cruelty and kindliness is often found in military commanders.

Roland H. Bainton

Chapter I.

AN APPROACH TO THE STUDY
OF THE PSYCHOLOGY
OF RELIGIOUS GENIUS

There is scarcely to be found a subject within the domain of psychology that presents a field for study which is more fascinating, and nevertheless important, than the study of the human personality. An inviting and important field and still, except for brief excursions, hardly charted. And how boldly this factor of human personality stands out in historical relief, immeasureable and indeterminable in terms of its background! Especially so is the case of those great religious personalities whose spirits stalk along through the centuries and whose imprint has been stamped into a universal inheritance.

There is scarcely to be found among history's greater personalities, a more unique and interesting character than that of "Martinus Ludher ex Mansfeld." Perhaps there is no biography that offers such opportunity for the study of the problem and power of personality as is his, a biography of rich and varied contrasts, set down and revealed in the voluminous products of his tongue and pen. To stand before him is to stand in the presence of a great religious genius. To follow his turbulent career is to pursue one who "trod like a giant through his age, tramping to earth what a thousand years had held in veneration" and to find that "everywhere new life blossomed in his footsteps".[1]

Great men will always present themselves in perennial interest to the student of mental life. What makes for a great personality? What, for genius? Whatever answer is given certainly cannot be stated in physical terms alone: if so, the problem would be less a problem to-day with our tremendously advancing knowledge of physical sequences (eugenics would then perhaps have a formula). We are here dealing with a problem whose complexity is concomitant with those subtle conflicts and co-ordinations of psychic life which together get expressed in personality and less frequently in genius. Some, indeed, are veritable optimists as they grapple with the problem of great personalities to refer all the factors to natural causes alone (known or unknown) as e.g., "It is quite certain that the whole of a man's life is accounted for by natural causes, the elements of his heredity and environment, but at present so large a portion of these forces are and must remain unknown, that we are forced to act in the maxim somewhere ennunciated by William James 'The originality of man does not date from something anterior; on the contrary certain other things date from it.' "[2]

This study offers little encouragement to

such optimism that hopes to refer the case of Religious Genius alone to factors in known natural causes plus unknown natural causes; but it does hope to present an optimism of such a character as will urge students of mental life to seek for a helpful solution to the problems of personality and genius in a certain direction, a direction, we think, that will reveal many of the hidden factors which ought to be revealed as constitutive and in a great measure determinative in the make-up of great men. We believe it to be a false optimism to hope to find all the factors which go to make up our Religious Genius and a false pessimism which holds that he is to be understood apart from any constitutive factors of his own psychic life.

We offer the Personality of the Great Reformer as an interesting and compelling contribution to the study and interpretation of the psychological problem of religious genius; and we would in this study present what we believe to be the inherent and determining factors which together were so co-ordinated and expressed as to make him the man of the hour and the hero of all times. Ours is an excursus in the study of the psychology of religious genius through a very notable biography.

The direction which offers considerable light in the interpretation of religious genius is that of the constitutive factors which make up the human self and which are expressed in personality. Each of us, retrospectively, may see

in our psychic life a history of unities and dis-
unities, chords and discords. Our mental life
is not a smooth-flowing stream with a straight
water-course down the years of experience, but,
contrariwise, more or less turbulent with many
a turn and even a tragic water-fall. A sketch of
the human self will reveal an uneven series of
duplicities and integrations, conflicts and
syntheses. Says Prof. James: "There are facts
which make us believe that our sensibility is
altering all the time, so that the same object
cannot easily give us the same sensation over
again.—The difference of the sensibility is shown
best by the difference of our emotion about the
things from one age to another, or when we are
in different organic moods.—Often we are ourselves struck at the strange differences in our
successive views of the same thing.—Experience is remoulding us every moment—our
brain changes—its whole internal equilibrium
shifts with every pulse of change.—I am aware
of a constant play of furtherances and hin-
drances in my thinking, of checks and releases,
tendencies which run with desire, and tendencies which run the other way.—The mutual
inconsistencies and agreements, re-inforce-
ments and obstructions, which obtain amongst
these objective matters reverberate backwards
and produce what seem to be incessant reac-
tions of my spontaneity upon them, welcoming
or opposing, appropriating or disowning,
striving with or against, saying yes or no."[3]

The constitutive factors which make up the human self and which are expressed in personality are in all of us, normally, complex, alternating and sometimes relatively unrelated. It sometimes makes us wonder whether we are one, two, or more selves. The experience of the Apostle Paul is a classic moral and religious expression to the struggles and conflicts of the self: "For the good which I would I do not: but the evil which I would not, that I practice—I see a different law in my members, warring against the law of my mind, and bringing me into captivity—wretched man that I am."[4] Or in the words of a modern religious writer: "Is not every man conscious of a strange duality, so that he seems two men? There is the self who is proud, envious, jealous—a lower self. There is the self which is modest, generous, ungrudging—a higher self."[5]

Literature is replete with such confessions of conflicts and contradictions.[6] The most potent and characteristic fact about the self is the continual play of mutations within it.[7] In all of us, as normal individuals, there are ceaseless alterations and recombinations of the self in response to the variety of situations which call them into activity. We see these "cross-currents" in our own altered feelings of well-being with feelings of depression. The most beautiful spring day may be for us the gloomiest without any apparent and challenging reason, or even during a festive hour when we are bubbling

over with a sense of exhilaration we may be
seized with a cruel sense of pessimism and depression which comes like an unexpected and
overwhelming tyrant to usurp and to subdue.

In short, there are cross-currents in all of us.
Browning interpreted these philosophically
and ethically in "Fifine at the Fair" in these
words: "It is when the struggle begins within
himself that man's worth something." But for
co-ordinating and integrating factors we might
all of us be of the homo duplex type, multiple
personalities, or dissociated selves. Abnormal
Psychology has contributed greatly to the
study of such phenomena.[8] These abnormal
persons suffer complete dissociations of their
cross-currents; the factors of their selves are
split off and lack integration. Their duplicities
are completely disintegrated so that when one
factor gains supremacy, the others lie dormant
and cut-off until the person assumes practically
a new role.[9]

The religious genius is one who has marked
strains in his personality, noticeable cross-
currents which play in constant struggle, but
who has the capacity to integrate and co-ordi-
nate these contradictions and duplicities into
a unity, a unity which has been deeply enriched
by the great play of undercurrents which persist as substructure to that self. It is from this
direction we would approach the study of the
genius of Martin Luther whose biography presents a rich field to such an interpretation. His

greatness in a surprising degree lies in the rich substructure of his self; a self full of contradictions, inconsistencies and cross-currents.

In the biographies of ordinary men the currents are less disturbing and challenging; in the religious genius they are powerful and assertive and play a part almost distressing. In the biographies of ordinary men the integrating factors which hold the self in a consistent whole are to be seen in deep-going lines of organization that are fairly constant and stable and which are held together by ordinary ties of habit, vocation, custom, etc. In the religious genius it takes an integrating factor more powerful than ordinary social customs, habits, etc., to hold the reins of the turbulent steeds of these cross-strains together; in most cases it requires a definite personal experience and self-appropriation before the necessary co-ordination is effected. That experience, be it found by vision, by mystic contemplation, by a tragedy, through a Book or a verse in the Book, must be large and powerful enough to hitch to a common post somehow all those struggling selves into a higher and a common relationship, which, if not accomplished, will result not in genius but in a pathological Duplex or perhaps Multiplex.

The account of Luther's career with its amazing variety of interests and accomplishments can only be understood by a study of Luther, the man. The account of the man is the record

of such interplay of cross-currents as suggested
above. His is a history of a civil conflict, desperate and almost the undoing of the man. His
self was so constituted that the ordinary co-
ordinating factors which provide unity in the
common man were for him by far insufficient.
His co-ordination could not be effected and be
satisfied with such as were presented by his
time and as given by the prevailing systems
and customs. His type demanded a new knot. It
is such with all men of genius: their needs reach
out and beyond the traditional. Comparing him
with other men struggling with their peculiar
strains, Prof. F. A. Christie remarks: "It is true
that many men, perhaps all men who have any
spiritual life, have at times felt the severity of
the war of the members against the spirit, the
great paradox of wanting to do that which one
hates. The annals of monasticism are full of
such men, who rolled in snow and lashed themselves with thorns to keep the body under. But
it is doubtful whether anyone ever felt the conflict more keenly than did Luther.—To those who
realize what the struggle cost him, his repeated
assurances that his public battles with princes
and false brethren were easier than his inward
struggles with the flesh and the devil, seem
perfectly natural."[10]

The study of the multiple elements which un-
derlie the self and which get expressed in personality is the approach we offer to the study
of the psychology of religious genius. The

autobiography gleaned here and there from the garrulous tongue and the busy pen of Luther will serve as a study in case. The greatness of this sixteenth century Protestant lies hidden away in those restless cross-currents which compelled him by his very mental constitution to seek a fresh synthesis and in the pursuit to launch out into new and unbeaten paths for satisfaction. We turn now to the study of some of these cross-currents.

NOTES AND REFERENCES

[1]Reinhold Seeberg, *Text Book of the History of Doctrines,* Trans. by C. E. Hay (Philadelphia: The United Lutheran Publication House, 1905), Vol. II, p. 221.

[2]Preserved Smith, "Luther's Early Development in the Light of Psycho-Analysis," *American Journal of Psychology,* 24, p. 360.

[3]William James, *Psychology* (New York: Henry Holt & Co., 1910), pp. 232, 233, 234, 299.

[4]Romans 7:19, 23, American Version.

[5]Ian Maclaren, *The Mind of the Master,* p. 120.

[6]Dr. George Matheson's analysis of the personality of the Apostle Peter is another case in point: "It very often happens that the men and women we meet in this world who seem most open and above-board are precisely those who prove the most difficult to read. Simon Peter is one of these—at the close of our inspection we find ourselves entangled in what appears to be a web of inconsistencies from which there is no hope of extrication. We seem to be confronted by a life of opposing qualities—sometimes

touching the heavens, at others coming periously near the nether world—now in the heights of ecstacy, anon in the depths of despair—today winning our admiration, tomorrow exciting a feeling akin to repulsion. The life, in fact, alternates between cowardice and bravery. We see him for an instant on the top of the wave, daring a deed which none of his compeers could have dared; the next he is shrinking with abject terror, 'Lord, save me!'

"Again I say I fail to recognize an adequate outward cause for the change. The cause, whatever it is, is *within* the man. His soul is a battlefield between bravery and cowardice: and here contend for the mastery of his heart the most opposite things in life.—Here, then, is a subject for the psychologist. We want to know why it was that within the soul of this man there could dwell such conflicting elements. We can understand a mixture of doubt and faith, we can imagine a union of weakness and strength, we can comprehend the existence of a natural placidness side by side with the possibility of flashing fire; but the co-existence of bravery and cowardice, the union of the hero and the faint-heart—that is something which challenges the philosopher and calls for explanation." *The Representative Men of the N.T.*, pp. 89, 90, 91, 92.

[7]Cf. James, *Psychology, op. cit.*, Chapters IX-X.

[8]Janet, *"L'Automatisme psychologique"* Lucie, Louise, Leouse. M. Prince, *The Dissociation of a Personality.* Beers, *A Mind That Found Itself.*

[9]Cf. Edwin D. Starbuck, "Double-Mindedness." *Encyclopedia of Religion and Ethics.*

[10]*Harvard Theological Review,* April, 1912, p. 243.

Chapter II.

CROSS-CURRENTS IN THE PERSONALITY OF MARTIN LUTHER

It is not from the point of view of a genetic study of his personality that we would consider the cross-currents in Martin Luther. This would indeed be an interesting chapter in itself. Ribot points out that there is compelling evidence of "successive contradictory characters" in the Reformer with very marked dividing lines as e.g., his so-called "first-conversion" which brought him from legal and secular studies into the retreat of a monastery; his so-called "second conversion" which freed him from the terrors of the Catholic penitential system and recreated him through a deep-seated experience to a new life of religious peace (synthesis) and assurance of salvation as expressed in the material principle of the Protestant Reformation "the just shall live by faith".[1] It is rather from the point of view of the "simultaneous" contradictory natures in him, we would concern ourselves; contradictions not confined to special periods in his genetic experiences but which occur and renew themselves throughout his life and which continually contribute as constitutive factors in his personality.

Among the noticeable and easily distinguish-
able simultaneous cross-currents in Luther's
personality we may profitably consider the following contradictory strains:

1. Self-Exaltation   —   Self-Abnegation
2. Cruelty   —   Kindliness
3. Humor   —   Melancholy
4. Practical-Temper   —   Mysticism
5. Critical-Temper   —   Superstition

These antithetical strains appear and re-appear
and to the consideration of these struggling
currents in his mental-life we now turn.

Section 1.   Self-Exaltation—Self-Abnegation

That Luther has by some been styled as an
egotist is due to the great strain of "self-exaltation" and his strong sense of personal consciousness. It gave him the self-confidence so
necessary to a thinker and leader. It made him
a born-innovator, a fearless antagonist to the
overwhelming powers of the hierarchical religious system with which it was his fate to deal
so strenuously. At times this strain asserts itself to the point wherein he would seem to be
worthy to lose any admiration and following.
But without it, he would have lain helpless as
a pawn before the bishops and the towers of his
religious environment. Conscious of his humble lineage he remarked with a sense of pride
and comfort:

Rich folks' children seldom turn out well.

They are complacent, arrogant, and conceited, and think they need to learn nothing because they have enough to live on, anyway. On the contrary, poor men's sons must labor to lift themselves out of the dust and must endure greatly. And because they have nothing to boast about or pride themselves upon, they trust God, control themselves, and keep still. The poor fear God, therefore He gives them good heads that they may study, become educated and intelligent, and be able to assist princes, kings, and emperors with their wisdom.[2]

Luther was not unconscious of his talents, the reward to poor men's sons! Throughout his immense correspondence he ever and again reveals the sense of satisfaction to the point of self-exaltation the progress he has been making in his studies and learning, and delights to pit his talents with any and all comers. "He never hesitated to boast of his knowledge of philosophy (e.g.) in contrast with the ignorance of his contemporaries, friends and foes alike."[3] Of course, he had the right of this self-consciousness and comparison, but the point is that it gave him a keen sense of pleasure, a kind of self-exhilaration which invoked in him a fearless and imposing disposition. Fanning this sense of pride over these talents were the recognition and applause of his student friends and contemporaries. He was known as "The Philosopher" among his companions at school. "He once remarked boastingly that if he had studied

law two years he would have known more about
it than a certain famous lawyer of the day."[4]
Luther carried with him throughout his life in
vivid memory the remark made to him by the
father of one of his associates when he was com-
plaining of poor health and fearing an early
death: "Do not be afraid, my dear Baccalaureus.
You will live to be a great man." He remem-
bered these words and repeated them long
after.[5]

Being well-versed in Latin, he found cause to
complain (one time on a visit in Italy) of the
bad Latin of the Italian monks: "whom he condemned as a set of ignoramuses because, it may
be supposed, they spoke it otherwise than he!"[6]
Urged by others to take the degree of doctor of
divinity which he did (Oct. 18th 1512), he was
not at all reticent about speaking of the rights
and privileges appertaining to the degree, ap-
pealing to it in justification to his right to teach
and to expound, with a keen sense of pride and
satisfaction. "Who compelled the Lord to make
me a doctor? Since He did it of His own will, let
come what may."[7] One cannot help, in reading
his letters to John Lang at Erfurt (February and
May 1517), being suspicious of his feeling a bit
of the self-exaltative and with that of self-confidence in his general disposition of Aristotle,
Porphyry and the "Sentences." "The wretched
studies of our age" to be superceded by the
theology of the Wittenberg professors (among
whom he was leader):

—that ridiculous and ingenious blasphemer Aristotle. His propositions are so absurd that an ass or a stone would cry out at them. —My soul longs for nothing so ardently as to expose and publicly shame that Greek buffoon, who like a spectre has befooled the Church.—If Aristotle had not lived in the flesh I should not hesitate to call him a devil.—Our theology and St. Augustine prosper and reign here, by God's help. Aristotle is gradually tottering to a fall from which he will hardly rise again, and the lectures on the Sentences are wonderfully disrelished—[8]

I am preparing six or seven candidates for the master's examination, of whom, Adrian, is preparing theses to shame Aristotle, for whom I want to make as many enemies and as quickly as I can—[9]

A trait in an individual is often brought to light under the pressure of opposition. It is characteristic of human nature that it takes often but a spark to ignite a seemingly negligent factor, perhaps otherwise dormant, in personality. This is just what occurs when Luther finds himself set down by John Eck as an unlearned and clumsy dreamer, a tremendous challenge to one whose self-consciousness spoke otherwise! He writes to John Sylvius Egranus at Zwickau in March 1518 concerning John Eck:

—In his Obelisks he calls me a fanatic Hussite, heretical, seditious, insolent and rash, not to speak of such slight abuse as that I am dreaming, clumsy, unlearned, and that I

dispise the Pope. In short, the book is nothing
but the foulest abuse, expressly mentioning
my name and directed against my Theses. It
is nothing less than the malice and envy of a
maniac. I would have swallowed this sop for
Cerberus, but my friends compelled me to
answer it.—The more they rage, the more I
give them. I leave the doctrine they barked
at yesterday for one they will bark at more
fiercely to-morrow.—I vow there is hardly any
theologian or scholastic, especially at Leipsic, who understands one chapter of the
Bible, or even one chapter of Aristotle's
philosophy, which I hope to prove triumphantly if they give me a chance.[10]

Luther, impressed by the enthusiastic recep-
tion given his theses (attacking the indulgence
practice) betrays again the characteristic current with which we are dealing, when he writes:

In fourteen days the theses ran through all
Germany; for the whole world was complain-
ing of indulgences, especially as preached
by Tetzel. When all the bishops and doctors
were silent and nobody ventured to bell the
cat,—for the Dominican heresy-hunters had
frightened every one with the threat of the
stake, and Tetzel himself had persecuted
certain priests who had criticized his shame-
less methods,—then I became famous, because at last some one had appeared who
dared to take hold of the business—[11]

In somewhat similar vein he later wrote to his
colleague Melanchthon:

> Nothing new or wonderful is happening here, except that the city is full of my name, and everybody desires to see the Herostratus who has kindled so great a fire.[12]

It is not without a feeling of pride and the strain of self-exaltation that Luther speaks of his multifarious duties counting and enumerating them again and again—frequently ending his letters with a "more at another time, for now I am very busy" or in similar phrase—e.g.,

> Greeting. I need a couple of amanuenses or secretaries, as I do almost nothing the live-long day but write letters. I do not know whether on that account I am always repeating myself, but you can judge. I am convent preacher, the reader at meals, am asked to deliver a sermon daily in the parish church, am district vicar (that is eleven times prior), business manager of our fish-farm at Litzkau, attorney in our case versus the Herzbergers now pending at Torgau, lecturer on St. Paul, assistant lecturer on the Psalter, besides having my correspondence, which, as I said, occupies most of my time. I seldom have leisure to discharge the canonical services, to say nothing of attending to my own temptations with the world, the flesh and the devil. You see how idle I am!—I begin tomorrow to lecture on Galatians, though I fear the plague will not allow me to finish the course.—I hope the world will not come to an end when Brother Martin does—.[13]

I have not time to write all, as I am not only Luther but Bugenhagen and notary-public and Moses and Jethro and what not? All in all, Jack of all trades and master of none.[14]

I am head over ears in business—visitor, reader, preacher, author, auditor, actor, runner, debater, and what not![15]

He was not without a keen sense of pride when he thought and spoke of his publications. Commenting on them and the rapidity with which his pen worked, he said:

I do not wish to praise myself, but the work (the German translation of the Bible) speaks for itself. The German Bible is so good and precious that it surpasses all the Greek and Latin versions, and more is found in it than in all the commentaries, for we clear the sticks and stones out of the way that others may read without hindrance.[16]

Grace and peace. The only news I have to write, dear Wenzel, is that Zwingli has sent me his foolish book with a letter written in his own hand and worthy of his haughty spirit. So gentle was he, raging, foaming and threatening, that he seems to me incurable and condemned by manifest truth. My comprehensive book has profited many.[17]

My letters are not Ciceronian and oratorical like those of Geickel, but at least I have substance if not elegant Latin.[18]

I bring forth as soon as I conceive. First, I consider all my arguments and words diligently from every point of view, so that I have a perfect idea of my book before I begin to write.—But my enemies the papists and others burst forth and bawl whatever comes into their heads first.[19]

In 1527 Luther spoke of his Church Postils as the "best book I ever wrote—which, indeed, pleases even the Papists."[20] Speaking of Aristotle's "Physics" and "Ethics" he remarked: "I know the book inside out, for I twice have expounded it to my brothers, having rejected the usual commentaries."[21] He was not without a genuine sense of self-exhilaration when he stepped into the pulpit, as he remarked:

> I recently delivered a sermon on the ban (Sermo de virtute excommunicationes) in which, incidentally, I taxed the tyranny and ignorance of the common herd of sordid officials, commissaries and vicars. All my hearers exclaimed in surprise they had never heard such a sermon before—.[22]

Together with the evidence of his practical and homiletical nature as a teacher and as a man of the pulpit, we cannot fail to see in some such utterance as the following his sense of self-assurance rising to the pitch of self-exaltation:

> A preacher should bare his breast and give the simple folk milk, for everyday a new need of first principles arises. He should be diligent with the catechism and serve out only milk leaving the strong wine of high thoughts for private discussion with the wise. In my sermons I do not think of

Bugenhagen, Jonas, and Melanchthon, for
they know as much as I do, so I preach not
to these but to my little Hans and Lena and
Elsa.—[23]

The self-exaltative in Luther gave him confidence in public debate and polemics. He found
joy in battle. He was conscious of his powers.
The following extracts speak for themselves:

—I wanted to have a public debate on the
matter, but rumor anticipated it and stirred
up some officials, so that they induced my
Bishop of Brandenburg to send a messenger
to put off such a debate, which I have done
and still do, especially as my friends advise
it. See what a monster I am, since even my
attempts are intolerable—.[24]

I believe that you know about my coming
debate at Leipsic and all my other doings. I
am lecturing on the Psalter again, and the
students are enthusiastic. The town is full of
students. Rome burns to destroy me, but I
cooly laugh at her. I am told that a paper
Luther was publicly burned and cursed in
the Campo di Fiore. I am ready for their
rage—.[25]

You would scarcely believe how pleased
I am that enemies rise up against me more
than ever. For I am never prouder and bolder
than when I dare to displease them—.[26]

It is interesting to read what the Knights of
his Round-table have set down as records of
Luther's table-talk.[27] Bearing on our discussion of the self-exaltative element in Luther's

personality, we note some interesting passages:

—But I chiefly oppose and resist their (papists) doctrine; I affirm roundly and plainly, that they preach not the truth. To this am I called; I take the goose by the neck, and set the knife to its throat. When I can show that the papists' doctrine is false, which I have shown, then I can easily prove that their manner of life is evil.—The pope has taken away the pure word and doctrine, and brought in another word and doctrine, which he has hanged upon the church. I shook all popedom with this one point, that I teach uprightly, and mix up nothing else.—[28]

When a man first comes into the pulpit, he is much perplexed to see so many heads before him. When I stand there, I look upon none, but imagine they are all blocks that are before me.[29]

—But it is a hard matter for one who has some particular gift and quality above another, not to be haughty, proud, and presumptuous, and not to condemn others; therefore God suffers them that have great gifts to fall many times into heavy tribulations, to the end they may learn, when God draws away his hand, that then they are of no value—.[30]

—I advise my chaplains and ministers to complain at court of their wants, miseries, poverty, and necessities; for I myself preached concerning the same before the prince elector who is both good and godly, but his courtiers do what they please. Philip Melanchthon and Justus Jonas were lately called in question at court, for the world's sake; but they made this answer: Luther is old enough, and knows how and what to preach.[31]

When I was in Rome, a disputation was openly held at which were present thirty learned doctors besides myself, against the pope's power—.[32]

If I had not been a doctor, Satan had made me work enough to do. It was no slight and easy matter for one to alter the whole religion of popedom so deeply rooted. But I promised and swore in Baptism that I would hold Christ and His Word, that I would steadfastly believe in him and utterly renounce the devil and all his lies—.[33]

The world fancies that if only it were rid of me all would be well.[34]

The end of the world may now come, for all that pertains to the knowledge of God has now been supplied.[35]

Had I not been a Doctor, the devil would have given me much trouble, for it is no small matter to attack the whole Papacy and to change it.[36]

But together with an unmistakable sense of extreme self-confidence and self-assertiveness in fearless attacks upon existing traditions and conditions—exhilarated and quickened in polemics and theological battles—we find a great "check" in a nature thus endowed which seemed to keep this great personality from overt extremes and which pulled the strings of caution and held at bay that which may easily

have led to a fiery radicalism. His "self-exaltation" is an indisputable trait of his fiery nature
and led him on before the face of all-comers. It
gave him the sense of sufficiency and fearlessness so much needed to a leader in that trouble-
some and restless day. But his deep-seated
sense of an inadequacy, a current of sincere
humility, an inner-reflective temper, held him,
possessed him continually throughout his
stormy career to the consciousness of the seri-
ousness of the cause he represented, of a sympathy with the troubled souls about him and of
the need for a close companionship to the Lord
of their souls.

A resolute, passionate, self-exaltative nature
in him was coupled with a hesitant, serene and
self-abnegative disposition which expressed
itself in fervent prayer and intimate intercourse
with his God. The terms "by grace" and "by
faith" so frequent and so burning with him fell
in fitly with this expressive side of his personality. Coming out of the monastery of the strict-
est asceticism his sense of dependence and
insufficiency was deepened by an experience,
paid at a price which nearly cost him his life,—
the way to religious peace he had learned was
not through purchase but through submission
and acceptance.

It is without question that the lessons of
strict obedience to parents and to teachers and
overseers so forcibly taught him in his early
youth, both by rule and by rod, had left upon
him indelible impressions which may in part

throw light upon his later theological beliefs of complete submission (sola fide) and dependence upon divine grace; at any rate the submissive spirit within him, dominant at times, held him in check over against an otherwise assertive and domineering side of his nature. Throughout his life he showed himself susceptible to direction and guidance by this current in his personality, making him a good listener, learner, student, sympathetic companion and above all producing the type of character which in the midst of terrific avalanches against friend and foe and assaults against him, stopped to return to itself for self-reflection and self-consideration. In other words, this strain in his mental make-up is continually being expressed in self-introspection. He knew his own weaknesses and unlike many others was willing to admit and publicly proclaim them. He knew his limitations and did not hesitate to acknowledge them. His secret sins and overwhelming temptations were an open book through his open confessions. The moral nature of man to him was of itself nothing of which one could boast. "The longer we wash, the uncleaner we are" fell from his lips at an early age. In the presence of duty and privilege he acknowledged his inadequacy. Before the great emergencies which were to tax the best of any physical and mental constitution, he felt the awful weight upon his only too weak shoulders, physically, mentally and morally. "If I perish,

the world will lose nothing," he wrote to Spalatin before the approaching Leipsic disputation.
"The Wittenbergers by the grace of God, have
already progressed so far they do not need me
at all. What will you? I, worthless man that I
am, fear I may not be counted worthy to suffer
and die for such a cause. That felicity belongs
to better men, not to so vile a sinner."[37] The
humility in him was not sham.

Before the great and to him unexpected re-
ception and enthusiastic approval of his ninety-
five theses, the attack on the indulgence-prac-
tices, he recoiled with a consciousness of the
tremendous responsibility which was thrust
upon him and his own feeling of insufficiency.
He wrote:

> —then I became famous, because at least
> some one had appeared who dared to take
> hold of the business. But the glory of it was
> not agreeable to me, for I myself did not know
> what indulgences were, and the song threat-
> ened to become too high for my voice.[38]

In similiar vein, he wrote to Staupitz, his superior, as the storm of conflict gathered and in
which storm his voice was destined to play such
a conspicuous part:

> See how insidiously I am attacked. Every-
> where I am hedged about with thorns; but
> Christ lives and reigns yesterday, and to-day,
> and forever.—Pray for me that in this time
> of temptation I be not too joyful and too con-
> fident.[39]

A most remarkable expression of the self-abnegative in Luther's personality appears in a letter by him to Cardinal Cajetan. Remarkable in that it appears in the midst of the turbulent correspondence and interviews which passed between the great powers representing Rome and the new cause represented by his bold challenges. A letter of apology!

> Most reverend Father in Christ, I confess, as I have confessed before, that I was certainly too indiscreet, as they say, and too bitter and irreverent toward the name of the supreme Pontiff. And although I was most strongly provoked to this irreverence, nevertheless I now know I ought to have handled the case more modestly, humbly, and reverently, and not answered a fool according to his folly. I am most sincerely sorry and beg pardon, and I will make it known to the people from the pulpit, whenever I have opportunity, as I have already often done, and will henceforth take care to act and speak differently by the mercy of God—[40]

There is much more than mere polite formality underlying his salutation in the letter of dedication of his now famous "An Open Letter to the Christian Nobility of the German Nation Concerning The Reform of the Christian Estate" (1520). There is a touch of genuine pathos which one receives in reading these lines, revealing as they do, again, his sense of the bigness of the cause and his feeling of unworthiness in shouldering its responsibilities:

The time to keep silence has passed and
the time to speak is come, as saith Ecclesiastes. I have followed out our intention and
brought together some matters touching the
reform of the Christian Estate, to be laid before the Christian Nobility of the German
Nation, in the hope that God may deign to
help His Church through the efforts of the
laity, since the clergy, to whom this task
more properly belongs, have grown quite
indifferent.—I know full well that I shall not
escape the charge of presumption in that I,
a despised monk, venture to address such
high and great Estates on matters of such
moment, and to give advice to people of such
high intelligence.—I pray you, make my
excuses to the moderately intelligent, for I
know not how to earn the grace and favor of
the immoderately intelligent, though I have
often sought to do so with great pains—God
help us to seek not our own glory, but His
alone! Amen.[41]

It is not out of sheer forwardness or rash-
ness that I, a single, poor man, have undertaken to address your worships.—In this
whole matter the first and most important
thing is that we take earnest heed not to enter
on it trusting in great might or in human reason, even though all power in the world were
ours; for God cannot and will not suffer a
good work to be begun with trust in our own
power or reason. —Let us act wisely, therefore, and in the fear of God. The more force
we use, the greater our disaster if we do not
act humbly and in God's fear.[42]

—I think too that I have pitched my song

in a high key, have made many propositions
which will be thought impossible and have
attacked many things too sharply. But what
am I to do? I am in duty bound to speak. If
I were able, these are the things I should
wish to do—.[43]

Says Professor McGiffert, commenting upon
this passage of Luther's Address to the German
Nobility: "For all his lack of worldly knowledge
he had one merit not shared by all venturing
into unfamiliar fields. He recognized his own
ignorance."[44]

And in the midst of his sudden popularity as
thousands flocked to his banner, when the name
"Luther" was the theme and conversation of
the hour, when "nine tenths of all Germany
were on Luther's side,"[45] when "no books but
his were sold in Worms, and his picture was
everywhere to be seen, often with the Holy
Ghost hovering over his head,"[46] when "the
people thought him sinless and infallible and
attributed miraculous power to him,"[47] we
hear again the self-abnegative voice coming
from his solitude at the Wartburg:

I beg that my name may be passed over in
silence, and that men will call themselves
not Lutheran but Christian. What is Luther?
My teaching is not mine. I have been crucified for nobody. Saint Paul would not suffer
Christians to bear the name of Paul or Peter,
but only of Christ. How does it happen that
I, a poor stinking carcass, have the children

of Christ called after my unholy name? Not
so, dear friends! Let us root out party names
and call ourselves Christians, for it is Christ's
gospel we have.[48]

A very striking blending of the two cross-
currents under consideration in this great personality appears in a sermon delivered on
Monday after Invocavit preached at Wittenberg
in Lent, 1522:

Take myself as an example. I have opposed
the indulgences and all the papists, but never
by force. I simply taught, preached, wrote
God's Word; otherwise I did nothing. And
then while I slept, or drank Wittenberg beer
with my Philip (Melanchthon) and with Ams-
dorf, the Word so greatly weakened the papacy, that never a prince or emperor in-
flicted such damage upon it. *I did nothing;*
the Word did it all. Had I desired to foment
trouble, I could have brought great blood-
shed upon Germany. Yea, I could have started
such a little game at Worms that even the
emperor would not have been safe. But what
would it have been? A fool's play. I did nothing; I left it to the Word.[49]

The self-abnegative note expressed itself
again and again in a complete self-surrender
to what he deemed to be God's will and work, to
which he felt himself but a mere instrument in
effecting. For example, among his Coburg
letters:

—I rejoice with all my heart that your

Grace (Elector John), by the grace of God, has come out of the hell at Augsburg. Though the disfavor of men looks sour not only to God, but to the devil as well, we yet hope God's grace, already ours, will be still more richly with us. They are in God's hands as well as we, that is certain, and they will neither do nor accomplish anything unless He wills it. They cannot hurt a hair of our heads, or of any one's, unless God compels it. I have commended the cause to my Lord God. He began it; that I know. He will also continue it; that I believe. It is not in man's power to start or create such a doctrine. Since it is God's, and all depends on His power and skill, not ours, I will watch to see who they are that wish to oppose and defy God Himself. Let things go as they please, in God's name.[50]

What a sharp contrast to the frequent appeal to his intellectual accomplishments as guaranteed by his doctorate (referred to above) is the following confession:

I have studied diligently, but as yet I do not understand one word of the Bible. I have not yet passed the primary class, but I am always turning over in my mind what I know, and asking for comprehension of the decalogue and the creed. It irks me not a little, that I, a doctor, with all my learning should willy nilly stay in the class with my little Hans and Magdalene and go to school with them—.[51]

Likewise, "at the sight of his little children

seated around the table, he called to mind the exhortation of Jesus, that we must 'become as little children'; and then added,"

Oh! dear God! Thou hast done clumsily in exalting children—such poor little simpletons—so high. Is it just and right that Thou shouldest reject the wise, and receive the foolish? But God our Lord has purer thoughts than we have; He must, therefore, refine us, as said the fanatics; He must hew great boughs and chips from us, before He makes such children and little simpletons of us?[52]

Again:

The reader of the Scriptures should be a humble person, who shows reverence and fear towards the Word of God, who constantly says: "Teach me, teach me, teach me". The spirit resists the proud; even though they are zealous and preach Christ for a time without fault, nevertheless, if they are proud, God excludes them from the Church. Wherefore every proud person is a heretic, if not de facto, nevertheless, potentially. *It is, however, difficult for him who is richly endowed with talents not to be arrogant.* But those whom God has adorned with great gifts he leads into most severe temptations, that they may see how helpless they are. Paul bore a thorn in the flesh (II Cor 12:7) lest he become proud, and unless Philip (Melanchthon) (a sickly body) were thus afflicted he would have wonderful opinions. If James and Agricola (contemporaries) should be-

come proud and despise their teachers I
fear that there would be no getting on with
them. I know the insolence of Munzer,
Zwingli and Carlstadt. Pride drove the angel
from heaven, and it spoils many a preacher.
Therefore it is humility that we need in the
study of sacred literature.[53]

In a letter of Luther's to the Elector Frederic
and Duke John of Saxony (Wittenberg, July
1524) we have a significant example of the two
cross-currents, the self-exaltative and the self-
abnegative, expressed in quick succession. He
speaks of his humility, how real it was to him,
then boasts of it, boasts of his fearlessness before tremendous odds, then affirms his weak
spirit and then confesses his right to a feeling
of pride for his victories and his intellectual
accomplishments:

I cannot boast or shout defiance in such
lofty words. I am a poor, miserable man, and
did not begin so splendidly, but with fear and
trembling, as St. Paul himself confesses that
he did, (I Cor 3:6) though he too might have
boasted about a voice from heaven. How humbly I attacked the Pope, how I besought him,
how I made requests of him, as my first
writings show! In poverty of spirit I did what
this world-devouring spirit has never tried
to do, but right manfully and like a knight
he has so far avoided doing them and fled
from doing them; and now he boasts of his
timidity as a high and knightly deed of the

spirit. I went to Leipsic to debate before a highly dangerous assembly. At Augsburg I appeared without safe conduct before my worst enemy. I went to Worms to answer to the Emperor and diet, although I well knew that they had broken my safe-conduct and planned all manner of wiles and treachery against me. Weak and poor though I was there, yet this is what was in my heart: if I had known that there were as many devils aiming their shafts at me as there were tiles on the roofs, I would have ridden in.—Again, I have had to appear in a corner, before one or two or three, others deciding who and where and how. My poor, troubled spirit has had to stand free, like a wild-flower, determining neither time nor person nor state, nor manner nor measure, as St. Peter teaches.

—They use and enjoy the fruits of our victory—though they have not won this victory and have not risked their lives for it, but I have had to win it at jeopardy of life. I must boast, as St. Paul too had to boast, though it is folly and I would rather not have done it.— I know and am certain, by God's grace, that I am more learned in the Scriptures than all the sophists and papists, but so far God has graciously preserved me, and will preserve me, from the pride which would make me refuse to give answer to the most insignificant Jew or heathen, or anybody else. . . .[54]

One cannot fail even upon a superficial study of the personality of this great Reformer to be impressed by the inconsistency and the con-

tradiction which appear in the traits above
considered. A man of self-assurance rising to
self-exaltation and yet a man of a keen sense of
inadequacy and self-effacement. Without question he enjoyed the popularity and the success
of his endeavors, each new victory bringing
forth from him newer and bolder challenges
to the highest authorities of his day and at the
same time a check of hesitancy and fearfulness
to reversals due to the consciousness of his
limitations and insufficiency before such
mighty undertakings. Amidst the satisfaction
that came with his many attending and exact-
ing duties, "eleven times prior," business manager, attorney, lecturer, preacher, correspon-
dent, etc., etc., to which he pointed frequently,
and amidst the joy of refutation and argument,
and the popularity in the school room ("I vow
there is hardly any theologian or scholastic,
especially at Leipsic, who understands one
chapter of the Bible, or even one chapter of
Aristotle's philosophy which I hope to prove
triumphantly if they give me the chance"),
—there falls from his lips such self-imposed
epithets as "a poor, offensive worm of the dust":
"I, a poor stinking carcass"; "I, worthless
man that I am"; "I a despised monk"; "so vile
a sinner"; "Christi lutum (Christ's mud)"[55];
a confessed ignoramus "I have studied diligently, but as yet I do not understand one word
of the Bible. I have not yet passed the primary
class—"! Defiant and aggressive yet cautious

and hesitant! Learned and yet foolish! Independent and yet dependent! Blessed with talents yet possessing none. Proud yet humble! Self-exaltative and yet self-abnegative!

Section 2.   Cruelty—Kindliness

We have already written, in connection with the self-exaltation in Luther's personality, of the fiery and the passionate in his nature. Self-assertiveness, aggressiveness, resoluteness coupled with action, is but an open door to boldness, combativeness and open invective. Fierce opposition and intolerance were the stones of the wall against which he was to hammer—and single-handed! There was no place for the weak in such a fray. A tradition of a thousand years of veneration is far from malleable; it is set and obstinate. Indeed "It was no slight and easy matter for one to alter the whole religion of popedom so deeply rooted." A leader at this period could only be found in a temper leaning towards pugnacity. Early in Luther's career we find him, a young monk as he was, boldly calling his brethren to task for their general laxity in observing the rules of fasting. It is reported that on one occasion when he tarried overnight at a certain convent in Italy as guest, that his fearlessness and invective almost cost him his life. As district vicar he was a strict disciplinarian over his brethren. One cannot but feel a certain callousness of his temper as he ruled over a fallen brother:

It is difficult for me to advise you what to do with him, for I am ignorant of your statutes. If they do not provide life imprisonment or capital punishment for such a crime, it seems to me he should receive as severe a penalty as they allow, for it is not you who punish, but justice and law, whose minister, not lord, you are. Do not be dissuaded by the fact that you are as great a sinner or a greater. It is enough to confess this to God. But here for the sake of edification we must nearly always punish those better than we, teach those more learned, rule those more worthy.— Therefore preserve humility and gentleness of heart toward him, but treat him rigorously(!!).[1]

His independence to existing practices is early seen as he hurled an almost sacrilegious invective against the custom of the day of making religious pilgrimages. It is the gradual awakening of a great Reformer:

If you have a wife, or servants who claim they are driven by the Spirit to go upon a pilgrimage, hear my advice: take a good oaken cross and sanctify them with a few lusty strokes on the back, and you will see how the devil is exorcised by this finger of God.[2]

In 1517 he addressed a letter to John Lang at Erfurt cursing Aristotle, Porphry and the dogmatic theologians who emphasized human ability and free will instead of the impotence of man and his need for divine grace. He insis-

ted that his old teacher, Trutvetter, read these
his invectives, since he had been taught at Erfurt to respect reverently these philosophies. It
was again a break with the popular philosophy and with his otherwise respected professors:

> I enclose a letter, dear Father (John Lang)
> for the excellent Trutvetter, containing pro-
> positions directed against logic, philosophy,
> and theology, i.e. slander and malediction of
> Aristotle, Porphry, and the "Sentences," the
> wretched studies of our age—that ridiculous
> and injurious blasphemer Aristotle. His
> propositions are so absurd that an ass or a
> stone would cry out at them.—My soul longs
> for nothing so ardently as to expose and
> publicly shame that Greek buffoon, who like
> a spectre has befooled the Church.—If
> Aristotle had not lived in the flesh I should
> not hesitate to call him a devil—[3]
> In the Universities the Bible and Chris-
> tian faith are little taught, and only the blind
> heathen Aristotle reigns. It pains me greatly
> that the damnable, proud, cunning heathen
> has led astray and fooled so many of the best
> Christians with his false words. God has
> plagued us with him because of our sins.[4]

Hurling an invective against the office of
bishop he said:

> Those happy times are gone by when it
> was a fortunate thing to be a bishop. Now
> there is no more miserable place, with its
> revelling and carousing after the manner of

> Sodom and Rome.—The best of them are im-
> mersed in public wars, while their homes
> have become a very hell of insatiable greed![5]

Independent we see him in his judgement. Independent of traditional practices, of former teachers, of "the presiding genius of mediaeval scholasticism (Aristotle)," independent of the sanctities which hovered over the name of ecclesiastical offices, he submitted to no one. An appeal to the pope against the indulgence practices not satisfying him, he was ready to break with that authority; at Augsburg he appealed from "the pope-ill-informed" to the "pope-to-be-better informed." Not gaining satisfaction he appealed to council. When council spoke against him he took his stand upon the Scriptures. But even here was not to be found the final word since not the whole of it taught Christian truth, and must be read with discrimination. And so he returned to himself and appealed to an enlightening Christian conscience. In all this we see him stepping forward in lively steps hurling thunderbolts to any and all, friend or foe, who stood in his way. He minced no words. The scythe of his tongue swept the field before him. Everything, no matter how much respected by time or age, must pass severe criticism and judgement before his own developing religious experience. As above stated, the type of leade needed for reform in these dark days—for they were dark—was not a weakling and a compromiser but a fearless antagonist and in every sense a reformer.

With a lively German tongue and violent pen, expressing a fiery and passionate nature we hear him thundering against a thousand different obstacles in terms which to-day might be provocative to a suit of libel. His violent epithets and polemics have been excused by his admirers as but common modes of expression characteristic of his day and age. But, as Professor McGiffert rightly remarks, "Though his form of expression might have been different in another century, the man he was would have been violent and vituperative in any. Passionate and high-tempered, to speak or write calmly about an antagonist was an impossibility to him."[6]

To set down "cruelty" as an expressive and open trait of his personality is not to misjudge or to misinterpret Luther. Evidences without number throughout his interesting career only strengthen such a character analysis. The self-exaltative, the sensitive, the assertive, the aggressive, the bold, the combative, the independent in his mental make-up were, together with a high-tensioned and a high-strung nervous constitution, but prophetic to such expressions of callousness, exaggeration, intolerance, vehemence and cruelty, such as we find in him.

"That I am vehement is not to be wondered at" he once remarked to a friend. "If you were what I am you too would be vehement." Again he remarked that anger oftentimes refreshed him like a thunderstorm and his pen therewith became unusually productive under its spell. Looking back upon some of the cruel and scathing invectives of his pen, late in his life he remarked: "I have read my book over again, and wonder how it happened that I was so moderate. I ascribe it to the state of my head, which was such that my mind was prevented from working more freely and actively."[7] "His violence," remarks Professor McGiffert, "was not merely a matter of temperament but also of deliberate choice."

As he once remarked, when criticized for his sharp words: "Our Lord God must begin with a pelting thunderstorm, afterward it rains gently and so soaks into the ground. A willow or hazel twig you can cut with a bread-knife, but for a hard oak you must have an ax and then you can hardly fell it and split it."[8]

In a letter to Spalatin in Feb. 1520, he justifies his vehemence upon the ground that it was necessary to advance the cause and that it was the natural expression of his nature:

Greeting. Good Heavens! Spalatin, how excited you are! (Spalatin had tried to calm Luther down!)—You do not see that my long suffering in not answering five or six wagon-loads of Emser's and Eck's curses was the sole cause why these bloated makers of placards dared to revile me with their ridiculous folly.—I despise their suspicion, reproaches, injuries and malices. Forsooth must we allow these bold men to add to their other furious acts the publication of libels, stuffed not only with lies, but with blasphemy against the gospel truth? Do you forbid us even to bark against these wolves? The Lord is my witness, how much I have restrained myself for the sake of the bishop's name, not to treat this cursed and impotent edict irreverently. I shall say elsewhere what their brains ought to hear—I consider them unpeaceable and in a future tract shall not abstain from treating them as violators of law, gospel and common sense, so they may know how much I have hitherto spared their ignorance and malice.—If you think properly of the gospel, please do not imagine that its cause can be advanced without tumult, offence and sedition.—Yet I cannot deny that I have been more vehement than I should; but as they know that I would be, they should not have irritated the dog. You know yourself how hard it is to moderate an angry pen.—*I am naturally warm,* and have a pen which is not at all blunt. So I am carried beyond the bounds of moderation by these monsters.[9]

Likewise:

—There is nothing new here except your picture-book on the Papacy. I approve of my picture with the sickle, for it shows that it was long ago foretold that I would be sharp and bitter, but I doubt whether the rose can be interpreted as an emblem of myself; I should think it applies rather to my office—.[10]

The tendency for such a choleric nature is to seek expression and Luther is no exception. In a letter to George Spalatin, the same day that together with the professors and the large concourse of students saw the burning of the papal bull and the canon law, Luther reveals a sense of satisfaction and peace in this expression of violence and public defiance:

Wittenberg, December 10, 1520

Greeting. In the year 1520, December 10, at nine o'clock, at the eastern gate, near the Church of the Holy Cross were burned all the papal books, the "Decretum," the "Decretals," "Liber Sextus," the "Clementines," the "Extravagantes," and the last bull of Leo X; likewise the "Summa Angelica," with some books of Eck and Emser and others which sundry persons threw on. *We did it* to show the incendiary papists that it took no great power to burn books they could not refute. This is my news.—Farewell.

Martin Luther[11]

The following passages speak for themselves on the trait under consideration:

Luther to Wenzel Link at Nuremberg

(Wittenberg) June 14, 1528

Grace and peace. You know more of the news than I can write you. You see what a commotion this confederacy of wicked princes has caused.—May God confound the worst of fools, who like Moab, is bold beyond his power and proud beyond his strength, as he has always been. *We shall pray against* these murderers. Hitherto we have spared them, but if they try anything again, we shall pray God and *advise our princes to destroy them without mercy,* for those unsatiable blood-suckers will not rest until they see Germany dripping with blood.—Farewell, and pray for us.

Martin Luther[12]

When I am dead I shall be a ghost to plague bishops and priests and godless monks, so that they will have more trouble with one dead Luther than with a thousand living.[13]

Lord, shield us with thy word and hope
And smite the Moslem and the Pope.[14]

So this Sodomite Pope, founder and master of all sins, threatens the Emperor Charles with excommunication and accuses him of sin, although he knows that his villainous tongue lies herein. These damnable rascals persuade the world that they are the heads of the Church, the mother of all churches, and masters of faith, although even stones and stocks would know that they were desperately lost children of the devil, as well as gross, stupid, ignorant asses in the Bible. One would like to curse them, so that thunder and lightening would smite them, hell fire burn them, the plague, syphilis, epilepsy, scurvy, leprosy, carbuncles, and all diseases attack them; but they are simple slanderers, and God has anticipated us and cursed them with a greater plague mentioned in Romans

1,26, to wit, that they become so mad that they know not whether they are men or women—.[15]

It seems to me, if the fury of the Romanists goes on in this fashion, no remedy is left except for emperor, kings, and princes to arm themselves and attack these pests of the whole world, and settle the affair no longer with words, *but with the sword.* For what do these lost men, deprived even of common sense, say? Exactly what was predicted of anti-christ, as if we were more irrational than blockheads. If we punish thieves with the halter, brigands with the sword, heretics with fire, why do we not still more attack with every sort of weapon these masters of perdition, these cardinals, these popes, and all this crowd of Roman Sodom, who corrupt the church of God unceasingly? Why do we not bathe our hands in their blood that we may rescue ourselves and our children from this general and most dangerous conflagration?[16]

Is not the above passage the expression of a cruel nature which, aroused, gives its stamp of approval to open violence? What a merciless and a cruel hatred is revealed in the following letter!

To John Goritz at Leipsic
                    (Wittenberg) January 29, 1544
Grace and peace. Dear Judge and good friend!

I am informed that you have at Leipsic, as a guest, one who calls herself Rosina von Truchess, such a shameful liar as I have never seen the equal of. For she first came to me with that name, giving herself out to be a poor nun of noble family, but on inquiry I found she had deceived me. When I asked her about it and inquired who she really was, she confessed that she was the daughter of a citizen of Minderstadt, in Franconi who had been killed in the Peasants' Revolt. She said she had been forced to wander around and was a poor child and begged me to forgive her for God's sake and to pity her. I told her henceforth not to tell such lies and not to take the name of Truchess. But while I took her obedience for granted and thought she did as I bade, she played the harlot behind my back and foully deceived every one with the name Truchess. I found this out after she had left, and can only think she was sent me by the papists as an archwhore, desperate character, and sack of lies, who did all sorts of harm to my cellar, kitchen, and rooms, and yet no one can be held accountable for it. Who knows what else she planned to do, for I took her into my own house with my own children. She had lovers and became pregnant and asked one of my maids to jump on her body and kill the unborn child. She escaped through the compassion of my Katie; otherwise she would have deceived no more men unless the Elbe ran dry. Wherefore pray keep an eye on this Truchess, and make it your duty to inquire where she is, that this cursed harlot, this lying, thievish wretch be not tolerated among you. Protect the evangelic cause, oblige me, and beware of her devilish frauds, thefts, and impostures. I fear that if a strict inquiry should be made, *she would be found to deserve death more than once,* as so many witnesses have appeared against her since she left. I have written to show you what I know about this case, so that my conscience may not be burdened by having kept silence instead of having warned you against this damned, lying, thievish harlot. Now do what you like; I am excused. God bless you. Amen.[17]

The temper of the above letter is certainly related to the confession Luther made to his friend Justus Jonas in a letter; "I am almost bursting with wrath and indignation," earlier in 1530.[18]

The Knights of his Round-Table have set down in their Table-Talk interesting sentences bearing further upon this phase of his personality:[19]

The pope places his cardinals in all kingdoms—peevish milk-sops, effeminate and unlearned blockheads, who lie lolling in king's courts, among the ladies and women.[20]

—The pope is not God's image, but his ape.[21]

—Seeing the pope is antichrist. I believe him to be a devil incarnate—.[22]

—There are many that think I am too fierce against popedom; on the contrary, I complain that I am, alas! too mild; I wish I could breathe out lightning against pope and popedom, and that every word were a thunderbolt.[23]

—If I were as our Lord God and had committed the government to my son as he to his Son and these vile people were as disobedient as they now be, I would knock the world in pieces.[24]

—A preacher must be both soldier and shepherd. He must nourish, defend and teach; he must have teeth in his mouth and be able to bite and to fight.[25]

—The Pope is a cuckoo who gobbles the eggs of his Church and vomits the Cardials.[26]

—Friars are lice placed by the devil on God Almighty's furcoat, and Friar-preachers are the fleas of His shirt.—I believe the Franciscans to be possessed of the devil, body and soul.[27]

More than ten years after Luther's final break with Rome, he published a pamphlet entitled "Against the Traitor at Dresden" in which he said:

This shall be my glory and honor, and I will have it so, that henceforth they will say of me that I am full of bad words, of scolding and cursing against the papists. I have often humbled myself for more than ten years, and used the very best language, but have only increased their wrath, and the peasants have been the more puffed up by my supplications. Now, however, because they are obdurate and have determined to do nothing good, but only evil, so that there is no longer any hope, *I will hereafter heap curses and maledictions upon the villains until I go to my grave,* and no good word shall they hear from me again. I will toll them to their tombs with my thunder and lightning. *For I cannot pray without at the same time cursing.* If I say, "Hallowed be Thy name," I have to add, "Cursed, damned, reviled be the name of the papists and of all who blaspheme Thy name." If I say, "Thy kingdom come," I have to add, "Cursed, damned, reviled, and destroyed be the papacy, together with all the kingdoms of the earth, which oppose Thy Kingdom." If I say, "Thy will be done," I have to add, "Cursed, damned, reviled, and destroyed be all the thoughts and plans of the papists and of every one who strives against Thy will and counsel." Thus I pray aloud every day and inwardly without ceasing, and with me all that believe in Christ. And I feel sure that my prayer will be heard. *Nevertheless I have a kind, friendly, peaceable, and Christian heart towards every one,* as even my worst enemies know.[28]

What a contradiction! "For I cannot pray without at the same time cursing," "Cursed, damned, reviled, and destroyed be all the thoughts and plans of the papists—." "Nevertheless I have a kind, friendly, peaceable, and Christian heart towards every one as even my worst enemies know." Was Luther sincere in this last claim? Was he, in spite of all his cruelty, a kind, friendly, peaceable, and Christian heart?

To a consideration of his "kindliness" we
now turn, and shall indeed find that his claim
is justified and that in his choleric and violent
fits of temper which pressed him to a pitch of
callousness and cruel hatred, there was in him
a cross-current, deep, refining,—a quality
which may well arouse the envy of the finest
type of a Christian gentleman. We refer to the
other side of the man's nature, his gentle, kind,
sympathetic, loveable, and charitable disposition.

Recalling the letter Luther wrote concerning
a fallen brother, recommending the severest
discipline and punishment and without any
thought of mercy or possible repentance on
the part of the guilty one (pp. 61-62), we feel in
the following letter as if we are introduced to an
altogether different vicar, a big sympathetic
and loveable heart at once foreign to the cruel,
unsympathetic and callous Luther who ruled
punishment "for the sake of edification"; and
yet it is the voice, not of the "vituperative" (as
Professor McGiffert calls him) Luther, but the
voice of the gentle and warm-hearted Luther, the
merciful vicar:

(Letter to the Augustinian
prior in Mayence)

I am sorry to hear that a certain brother,
George Baumgartner, from one cloister in
Dresden, who fled, alas! because guilty of
shameful conduct, has taken refuge with
you. I thank you for your faithfulness and
kindness in receiving him, that the scandal

might be stopped. He is my lost sheep and
belongs to me; mine it is to seek him and to
restore the erring one, if it please the Lord
Jesus. So I beg you by our common faith in
Christ and by the order of St. Augustine that,
if you can, you will send him to me to Dresden or Wittenberg, or will lovingly persuade
him to return of his own free will. I shall receive him with open arms if he comes. He
need have no fear of my displeasure. I know,
I know, that offences must come, and it is no
marvel when a man falls, but it is a miracle
when he recovers himself and remains stead-
fast. Peter fell that he might know he was
human. To-day even the cedars of Lebanon
fall, though while they stand they reach the
heavens. Yes, even an angel in heaven fell—
a wonder it was indeed—and Adam fell in
paradise. So is it surprising the reed should
bend before the storm and the smoking flax
be extinguished?[29]

Is it the same Luther that ruled over Rosina
von Truchess? (See p. 71 ff.)

Again, recalling the letter of Luther to Spalatin in which he gave a brief account of the
burning of the bull and the other hated documents and in which letter he refers to himself
with satisfaction as one of the crowd: "We did it
to show the incendiary papists—" (cf. p. 68)
again, we wonder how, as in the following letter,
he could have been so cautious and considerate
and tender, referring to a similar outbreak and
in spite of the fact that at the time of its compo-

sition there was a tremendous avalanche of hostility already hurled against him:

Luther to John Lang at Erfurt.

Greeting.—The false preachers of indulgences are thundering against me in wonderful style from the pulpit, and as they cannot think of enough monsters with which to compare me they add threats, and one man promises the people that I shall certainly be burned within a fortnight and another within a month.—If rumor has perhaps told you anything about the burning of Tetzel's "Theses" lest anyone should add anything to the truth, as is usually the case, let me tell you the whole story. The students are remarkably tired of sophisticated and antiquated studies and are truly desirous of the Holy Bible; for this reason, and perchance also because they favored my opinion, when they heard of the arrival of a man sent from Halle by Tetzel, the author of the "Theses," they threatened the man for daring to bring such things here; then some students bought copies of the "Theses" and some simply seized them, and, having given notice to all who wished to be present at the spectacle to come to the market place at two o'clock, they burned them without the knowledge of the elector, the town council, or the rector of the university or of any of us. Certainly we were all displeased by this grave injury done to the man by our students. I am not guilty, but I fear that the whole thing will be imputed to me.[30]

It may be said that the different attitudes of Luther on these two occasions were due to a growing hostility which made him, later, to reverse his caution shown in this letter. True. And yet, the two traits revealed in these contradictory attitudes, may not be segmented into certain and definite periods of his life, but interplay and express themselves continually. The contradictions of these stands which he took are to a very great extent the expressions of the contradictory strains of "cruelty" and kindliness" in his mental make-up.

Luther admitted in a letter to Spalatin in 1520 that he wrote "much more vehemently against Emser, Eck and Tetzel" than to others, and yet the lashing of his tongue against Tetzel, did not drown out the tender and the forgiving in his nature, as is seen when, at the time of the breakdown in health of the indulgences-seller and hearing that John Tetzel, his foe, lay mortally ill, he wrote a letter of comfort and cheer and bade him "not to be troubled, for the matter did not begin on his (Tetzel's) account, but the child had quite a different father."[31] Is this not the expression of a big, generous, warm and kindly heart? We cannot fail to sense the man's bigness!

In the very heat of controversy, when his anger was aroused and heightened to a pitch of near-madness, he could suddenly turn to the writing of beautiful letters and tracts for the solace and the inspiration of the sick and suf-

fering; in the very midst of the stress and strain
of conflict, he could pause to make a kindly
pastoral call, offer spiritual consolation to a
sick one, administer the sacrament and pour
out a tender heart.[32] In the thick of opposition
there came forth from his pen edifying moral
and religious tracts, homilies and profound
papers of Biblical exegeses, containing no
trace whatever of the terrible mental strains
through which he was passing. Some of the
most beautiful and inspiring expressions of
his tender and sympathetic soul were given
birth in the heat of controversy!

"He was very human," writes Professor Mc-
Giffert, "this hero of ours, fiery-tempered,
passionate, imperious, lovable withal, warm-
hearted, and generous to a fault. Full of contradictions, he had the frankness and carelessness of genius, and what he was he showed, and
what he thought he said, without concealment
and diplomacy. Like a Cromwell or a Napo-
leon in his masterful will, he was like our own
Lincoln in his human sympathies, his simpli-
city of character, his transparent honesty."[33]
Further, "Despite the storm gathering about
his head, Luther went on as usual with his
regular work, paying no attention to his enemies' attacks and interesting himself in university affairs as if nothing uncommon had
happened. One of the extraordinary things
about the man was the way he could detach
himself from conflict even when it had grown

the hottest, and could teach and preach and write as if all were serene. Often when in the thick of the fight he would produce a scriptural commentary or a devotional work such as might be expected to come only from the pen of one whose whole life was spent in quiet study or in the calm of religious meditation; and this even after he had developed into one of the most active, vigorous, and unresting combatants the world has ever seen."[34]

This "detachment" which is certainly curious and wonderful in the man, can be explained only in the light of the other deeply grounded cross-current in his self, the tender, the kind, the sympathetic, the human, which brought him ever to return to himself and to the companionship of his friends and made him attentive to the needs about him. A man of his fiery type without this "pull" from powerful yet tender strings, could not have returned to and "detached" himself in such a remarkable way unless the tender and the warm in him were genuine and deeply rooted integrals of his personality.

On the "kindliness" and the warmhearted and the sympathetic in his personality, some such passages as these speak for themselves in stronger terms than mere character-analysis:

"As his daughter lay very ill, Dr. Luther said:

I love her very much, but dear God, if it be thy will to take her, I submit to thee.

Then he said to her as she lay in bed:

> Magdalene, my dear little daughter, would
> you like to stay here with your father, or
> would you willingly go to your Father yon-
> der?

She answered: "Darling father, as God wills."
Then he said:

> Dearest child, the spirit is willing, but the
> flesh is weak.

Then he turned away and said:

> I love her very much; if my flesh is so strong,
> what can my spirit do? God has given no
> bishop so great a gift in a thousand years
> as he has given me in her. I am angry with
> myself that I cannot rejoice in heart and be
> thankful as I ought.

Now as Magdalene lay in the agony of death,
her father fell down before the bed on his knees
and wept bitterly and prayed that God might
free her. Then she departed and fell asleep in
her father's arms.—As they laid her in the coffin he said:

> Darling Lena, you will rise and shine like a
> star, yea like the sun.—I am happy in spirit,
> but the flesh is sorrowful and will not be
> content; the parting grieves me beyond
> measure.—I have sent an angel saint to
> heaven.

Three days later he wrote to Justus Jonas:

> I believe that you have already heard that

my dearest daughter Magdalene has been reborn to the eternal kingdom of Christ; and although my wife and I ought only to give thanks and rejoice at such a happy pilgrimage and blessed end, whereby she has escaped the power of the flesh, the world, the Turk, and the devil, yet so strong is natural affection that we must sob and groan in heart under the oppression of killing grief. —Would that I and all mine might have such a death, or rather such a life. She was, as you know, of a sweet, gentle and loving nature."[35]

Luther to Nicholas Hausmann

Wittenberg August 6, 1528

Grace and peace. My little Hans thanks you, dear Nicholas, for the rattles. He is very proud of them and takes great pleasure in them. I had determined to write something about the Turkish war, but I hope it will be needless. My little daughter Elizabeth is dead. (Lived 8 months.) It is marvellous how sick at heart, *how almost womanish it has left me,* so much do I grieve for her. I would never have believed that a father's heart could be so tender for his child. Pray the Lord for me, and farewell.[36]

—Although it is market season here, I can find nothing in this city for the children. Have something on hand if I should fail to bring anything home for them.[37]

"Two little birds made a nest in Dr. Luther's garden and flew home in the evening, often frightened by passers-by; he called to them:

Oh, you dear little birds, do not fly away. I love you with all my heart if you could only believe me. But thus we also lack faith in our God."[38]

To my dear son, Hans Luther: Grace and peace in Christ my darling little son. I am very glad to hear that you are studying well and praying diligently. Go on doing so, my little son, and when I come home I will bring you a beautiful present.

I know a lovely, pretty garden where there are many children. They wear golden coats, and pick up fine apples, pears, cherries, and plums under the trees. They sing and jump and are very merry. They also have beautiful little horses with bridles of gold and saddles of silver. I asked the man who owned the garden who the children were. He answered, "These are the children who gladly pray and study and are good." Then I said, "Dear man, I also have a son named Hans Luther. Wouldn't he like to come into the garden and eat such beautiful apples and pears and ride such fine horses and play with these children!" Then the man said, "If he prays and studies gladly, and is good, he too shall come into the garden, and Lippus and Jost with him. And when they are all here they shall have whistles and drums and lutes, and all sorts of things to make music with, and they shall dance and shoot with little crossbows." And he showed me a beautiful meadow in the garden fixed for dancing. Gold whistles were hung there, and drums and silver crossbows. But it was still early and the children had not yet eaten, so I couldn't wait for the dance, and I said to the man: "Dear sir, I will go as fast as I can and write it all to my dear son Hans, that he may study and pray well and be good and so come into this garden. But he has an Aunt Lena whom he will have to bring with him." Then the man said, "Very well, go and write it to him."

Therefore, dear little son Hans, study and pray bravely, and tell Lippus and Jost to do so too, and you shall all come into the garden with each other. The dear God take care of you. Greet Aunty Lena and give her a kiss for me.

Your loving father,
MARTIN LUTHER

April 22, 1530.[39]

Indeed, do not these passages plainly reveal this strong trait of kindliness, tenderness, and deep sympathy in the Reformer, University Professor and father? It is well known how this trait found expression in Luther's own home. His reckless hospitality to all comers was known abroad in his day so that his home became the Mecca and stopping-off place of poor relatives, nephews and nieces, poor university students, needy priests, and stranded travelers. Besides his own children, Luther brought up no less than eleven of his orphaned nephews and nieces.[40] Conrad Cordatus (one of the reporters of the Table-Talk), after spending a number of years in wandering, and studying theology, finally found a kind refuge at Luther's table where he continued as a dependent. Cordatus became involved in frequent disputes with "Mrs. Luther" but the generous and sympathetic Professor continued to offer to him the hospitality of his home.

His household is described by George Held in 1542 as "inhabited by a miscellaneous and promiscuous crowd of youths, students, girls, widows, old maids and children, and very unrestful." He probably entertained his students gratuitously.[41] "There is never any mention of board bills in the Table Talk, and when Luther speaks of a financial transaction between a student and himself, the student is usually the beneficiary. Doubtless some of them, as Dietrich, Lauterbach, and Aurifaber, paid for their entertainment in services as secretaries. The relation of 'famulus' is one which has lasted to the present day, and is immortalized in the person of Faust's Wagner. Other students, as perhaps poor Schlaginhaufen, may have been taken for charity, and so expected to be ready to do odd jobs in return.—Luther's carelessness and generosity in money matters is well established—."[42] "Despite it all" again quoting Professor McGiffert, "the early years of his married life were full of money troubles. He was very free with what he had, giving away his last gulden without hesitation, and when there was no more money, tableware and house-

hold ornaments, presented to Käthe or himself
by admiring friends, would often go to relieve
the wants of the needy. He frequently complained humorously of his own soft-hearted-
ness and gullibility, lamenting that anybody
could take him in with a smooth story."[43]

Section 3. Humor—Melancholy

Johannes Mathesius, one of the company at
Luther's table, thus describes the Great Reformer as "von Natur ein hurtiger und frölicher
Geselle"[1] which expression is reemphasized
by his contemporaries and by his own letters
and documents. And yet the same Luther suffered perhaps as few of the heroes of literature
and of history from periods of utter despondency and despair. Speaking of his own experiences he confessed: "I know a man who has
often, though only for brief periods, suffered
the pains of hell such as no tongue or pen
could describe and no one could believe, if he
had not himself felt them. If they had lasted for
a half or even a tenth part of an hour, he would
have perished altogether and his bones would
have crumbled to ashes."[2] How that this was
no mere hyperbole and how that these periods
of despondency and despair were real visita-
tions in his life, we shall discuss later. It is well
to introduce this dark background and have it
continually before us in the presentation of the
jovial side of his nature in order to appreciate
these two tremendous cross-currents!

Had it not been for the lighter vein which formed a vital part of his personality, he would have been undone early in life. His melancholic nature needed a strong current of opposition to carry him on and to bear him over a possible psychopathic and disintegrating condition. What we may term the "humor" in him, genuine to the core, was the saving grace and the freeing agent from the stress and strain of a hyper-sensitive and self-conscious, self-reflective nature, plus the critical and the nerve-wracking circumstances and fierce opposition in which he was engulfed. Humor is often the safety-valve in a nature already overburdened with pressure.[3]

Perhaps two of the most intense and critical situations in which Luther found himself as a lone-prophet of a new era were the debate at Leipsic with the ablest German Catholic theologian of the day, 1519, and the memorable Diet of Worms, 1521. Anyone who appreciates the tremendous significance not alone for Luther but for the whole Protestant cause of these two occasions, would say that they were enough to tax the mental balance of the strongest soul. And so they were. But the genius that stood before the eager throng and before "the malignant foe" and that fearlessly relied himself to the unmistakable voice of his conscience, was literally borne and carried over these tense situations by the cooling and refreshing powers which gushed forth, unbidden, from the deep

wells of the humor-side of his great personality.

Among the most interesting of contemporary letters of this time is that of Peter Mosel-
lanus to Julius Pflug, giving us a description
of Luther at Leipsic:

> I see that you are desirous of learning the
> history of the cause of Martin the theologian.
> —I was present (at the Leipsic debate) by
> chance.—Men of every estate gathered to
> see the debate, abbots, counts, and knights,
> learned and unlearned, so that this large
> university had no hall big enough to accom-
> modate such an audience.—To prevent a
> tumult armed guards were stationed at the
> doors.—I will give you portraits of the lead-
> ers in this war. Martin is of middle height
> with slender body worn out both by study
> and care, so that you can almost count his
> bones. He is in the vigor of manhood; his
> voice is sharp and clear. He is so wonder-
> fully learned in the Bible that he has almost
> all the texts in memory. He has learned
> enough Greek and Hebrew to form a judg-
> ment of the translations. He has no lack of
> matter in speaking, for an immense stock of
> ideas and words are at his command. Per-
> haps you might miss in him judgment and
> method in using his stores. In daily life and
> manners he is cultivated and affable, having
> nothing of the stoic and nothing supercili-
> ous about him; rather he plays the man at all
> seasons. *He is a joker in society, vivacious
> and sure, always with a happy face no matter*

> *how hard his enemies press him.* You would
> hardly believe that he was the man to do
> such great things unless inspired by the
> gods.—[4]

It is related that, at Leipsic, Luther carried on
the platform with him a bouquet of flowers and
in the midst of his fiery disputation he would
pause now and then to refresh himself by smel-
ling the beautiful bouquet. Eck thundered!
Luther pauses now and then to find cheer and
companionship in the simple flower! Nothing
wrong about that, but is there not a quiet humor in the situation?[5]

Again, when Luther stands before the huge
and brilliant assembly of princes and nobles,
prelates and doctors, presided over by the
youthful Emperor Charles V, at Worms in
April, 1521, a moment as Carlyle calls it "the
greatest moment in the dawning period of humanity", there comes forth from his lips amidst
the solemnity of his final reply and stand, a
quiet bit of humor. Thundering and threatening were the speeches of his opponents. Luther
explains his stand. Eck accuses him of ambi-
guity and challenges him to give "a simple
unsophisticated answer without horns (non
cornutum)." The hero replies:

> Since your Majesty and your Lordships
> ask for a plain answer, I will give you one
> without either horns or teeth. (Neque cornu-
> tum neque dentatum). Unless I am convicted
> by Scripture or by right reason—unless I

> am thus convinced—I neither can nor will
> recant anything, since it is neither right
> nor safe to act against conscience. God help
> me. Amen.[6]

"Neque cornutum neque dentatum!" Eck meant, of course, "speak to the point, give us a definite answer." The playful in Luther is aroused! Like a flash there appears in his active mind a University campus scene: the figures, grotesque, of student masqueraders parading about the school-campus, wearing hoods upon which were fastened horn-like appendages, with ugly tusks and asses' ears fastened to them—the symbol of their Freshmen naiveté and ignorance—waiting for the solemn ceremony when the hood of ignorance was to be removed from them by their upperclass-men and when they should be declared eligible to the privileges of academic citizenship. Eck's word "cornutu" is taken up in a humorous setting by the University Professor. The reader may draw from the analogy his own conclusions. May we not imagine how the countenances of the audience must have lit up with this quick parry on Luther's tongue? Is it not the "humor" strain in him that is here ventilated in the tense situation at Worms?[7]

Writing about Luther before-the-Diet of Worms, Aleander, one of the formidable allies of the pope, said: "The fool entered smiling and, before the Emperor, kept his head turning continually hither and thither."[8] It is related

that the humanist Peutinger, a delegate from
the city of Augsburg, happened to be standing
near Luther at this significant occasion and
was greeted cheerily by the Reformer with
these words: "What, you here, too, Herr Doktor?"[9] Luther himself remarked about his
mood at Worms:

> The devil saw clearly the mood I was in
> when I went to Worms. Had I known as many
> devils would set upon me as there were tiles
> on the roofs, I should have sprung into the
> midst of them with joy.—I was undismayed
> and feared nothing, so foolish can God make
> a man! I am not sure I should now be so joy-
> ful.[10]

What is now known as "Luther's Coburg Letters" are replete with humor. At this time Luther
was under the Elector's protection against the
imperial ban and for more than five months
was in almost solitary confinement at the
powerful fortress of Coburg, 1500 feet above
sea level. (1530) From this high fortress there
radiated down a series of interesting Luther
documents which revealed to the world outside that the jocose spirit, in spite of the un-
certainties of his future, was far from dead. He
named his new place of abode his "Sinai" but
promised he would change it into a "Zion":

> To Philip Melanchthon (at Nuremberg?)
> The Realm of the Birds at Three P.M.
> (April 23, 1530)
> Grace and peace in the Lord Jesus. I have

come to my Sinai, dearest Philip, but I shall
soon make it a Zion and build three Taber-
nacles, one for the Psalter, one for the Pro-
phets, and one for Aesop—.[11]

To his table-companions at home, he wrote of
his new situation:

At the Diet of the Grain Turks, April 28, 1530.

Grace and peace in Christ. Dear Gentlemen
and friends—that you may learn how things
are with us, I would have you know that we,
namely Veit Dietrich, Cyriac Kaufmann,
and I, did not press on to the Diet of Augsburg,
but stopped to attend another diet here. There
is a coppice directly under our windows,
like a little forest, where the daws and crows
are holding a diet; they fly to and fro at such
a rate and make such a racket day and night
that they all seem drunk, soused and silly.
I wonder how their breath holds out to bicker
so. Pray tell me have you sent any delegates
to these noble estates? For I think they must
have assembled from all the world. I have
not yet seen their emperor, but nobles and
soldier lads fly and gad about, inexpressive-
ly clothed in one color; all alike black, all
alike gray-eyed, all alike with the same
song, sung in different tones of big and little,
old and young. They care not for a large
palace to meet in, for their hall is roofed with
the vault of the sky, its floor is the carpet of
green grass, and its walls are as far as the
ends of the worlds. They do not ask for horses
and trappings, having winged chariots to
escape snares and keep out of the way of

man's wrath. They are great and puissant lords, but I have not yet learned what they have decided upon. As far as I can gather from an interpreter, however, they are for a vigorous campaign against wheat, barley, oats, and all kinds of corn and grain, a war in which many a knight will do great deeds. So we sit here in the diet and spend time agreeably seeing and hearing how the estates of the realm make merry and sing. It is pleasant to see how soldierly they discourse and wipe their bills and arm themselves for victory against the grain. I wish them good luck—to be all spitted on a skewer together. I believe they are in no wise different from the sophists and papists who go for me with their sermons and books all at once; I see by the example of the harsh-voiced daws what a profitable people they are, devouring everything on earth and chattering loud and long in return.—[12]

Again, while at Coburg, he admonishes his friends to cultivate the virtue of cheerfulness:

—Whenever this temptation comes to you beware not to dispute the devil nor allow yourself to dwell on these lethal thoughts, for so doing is nothing less than giving place to the devil and so falling. Try as hard as you can to despise these thoughts sent by Satan. In this sort of temptation and battle contempt is the easiest road to victory; laugh your enemy to scorn and ask to whom you are talking. By all means flee solitude, for he lies in wait most for those alone. This devil is conquered by despising and mocking him, not by resisting and arguing. Therefore, Jerome, joke and play games with my wife and others, in which way you will drive out your diabolic thought and take courage.—

Be strong and cheerful and cast out these monstrous thoughts. Whenever the devil harasses you thus, seek the company of men or drink more, or joke and talk nonsense, or do some other merry thing. *Sometimes we must drink more, sport, recreate ourselves, aye, and even sin a little to spite the devil,* so that we leave him no place for troubling our consciences with trifles. We are conquered if we try too conscientiously not to sin at all. So when the devil says to you: "Do not drink," answer him: "I will drink, and right freely, just because you tell me not to." One must always do what Satan forbids. *What other cause do you think that I have for drinking so much strong drink, talking so freely and making merry so often, except that I wish to mock and harass the devil* who is wont to mock and harass me. *Would that I could contrive some great sin to spite the devil,* that he might understand that I would not even then acknowledge it and that I was conscious of no sin whatever. We, whom the devil thus seeks to annoy, should remove the whole decalogue from our hearts and minds.[13]

Preserved Smith, a profound Luther scholar, has this to say on the trait under consideration:

"No picture of Luther would be complete without making his humor conspicuous. He was as fond of a joke or a good story as was Abraham Lincoln; his letters and table-talk are as full of puns as are Shakespeare's plays. Like all puns they can only be appreciated in the original. But of his stories, many of them indeed old in his time, some specimens must be given, in order, as the old English translation of the table-talk puts it, 'to refresh and recreate the company'":—

Whatever one does in the world is wrong. It is with me as in the fable of the old man, his son, and the ass: whatever I do is wrong. One physician advises me to bathe my feet at bedtime, another before dinner, a third in the morning and a fourth at noon; whatever I do displeases some. So it is in other things; if I speak I am turbulent, if I keep silence I spit on the cross. Then Master Wiseacre comes along and hits the poor beast on the rump.

I am the father of a great people, like Abraham, for I am responsible for all the children of the monks and nuns who have renounced their monastic vows.

Women wore veils because of the angels; I wear trousers because of the girls.

Peasants are proudest of wealth and yet uncouth, as can be seen by the story of one who could not keep a fly from lighting on his spoon and so finally ate it with his food. Another rustic in Mansfeld had trouble in keeping a robin from perching on his bowl and so at last ate it alive, and when he heard it still chirping in his stomach, said, "So you keep on peeping, do you?" and poured down a schooner of beer to drown it.

A man was burned at Prague for teaching his dog to jump through a ring when he said "Luther." O Lord, how wondrous are thy ways!

Bugenhagen is Minos, Rörer Aeacus, and Crödel Rhadamanthus. They are one substance in three persons, Bugenhagen the Father, Rörer, the Son, and Crödel the Holy Ghost. They simply won't let me alone, I have to do the "Kyrie Eleison" for Crödel because he gave me three or four kegs of beer; Rörer orders me about the gospels and collects; and if Bugenhagen hears of some things I do, I shall have to leave.[14]

On January the 28th 1533, Luther's third son was born. The proud parent said the next day:

A new Pope has just been born; you will help the poor fellow to his rights.—I have called him Paul, for St. Paul has given me many good sayings and arguments, wherefore I wish to honor him.[15]

Again the playful in Luther:

The money I realized by the sale of the books you sent I have given, in accordance with your directions, to the poor—that is, to myself and the brethren, for I have never known anybody poorer than I.[16]

Luther's letters to his wife, his "Lord Katie," are tender, and oftentimes full of humor, e.g.,

To Catharine Luther at Wittenberg

(Dessau), July 29, 1534

Grace and peace in Christ. Dear Master Katie, I have nothing to write, as Melanchthon and others are going to Wittenberg and will tell you all the news. I must stay here for the sake of good Prince Joachim. Imagine if you can why I should stay so long or why you ever let me go. I think Francis Burkhardt would be willing to see me depart, as I would him. Yesterday I shipped some bad beer for which I had to sing out. There is nothing fit to drink here, for which I am sorry as I like it, and think what good wine and beer I have at home, and also a fair lady (or should I say lord?). It would be a good thing for you to send me the whole wine-cellar and a bottle of your own beer as often as you can. If you don't I shall not come back for the new beer. God bless you and the children and household. Amen.

Your lover,
MARTIN LUTHER.[17]

That Luther liked companionship and a rollicking good time, is evidenced by this letter to Justus Jonas, Sept. 4th, 1535 (Luther was preparing a banquet in honor of Jerome who was completing his studies for the doctorate);

Now our head cook, Lady Katie, begs you to take this thaler and buy us all sorts of birds and fowls of the air, and whatever else

is subject to man's dominion and lawful to
eat in the aerial kingdom of feathers—but
not crows. As to sparrows, God loves them
so that we would like to eat them all up. If
you spend more than this thaler—I'll give
it to you. Moreover, if you can buy or catch
—which would cost you nothing—any hares,
or such tidbits, send 'em on, for we are minded
to satisfy your stomachs for once, especially
if it can be done with malt liquor, as they
call it. My Lord Katie has brewed seven kegs
in which she put thirty-two bushels of malt,
hoping to gratify my palate. She trusts that
the beer will be good, but you and the rest
will find that out by testing it.—We shall
certainly live merrily if you come to us
with all those winged creatures, whom we
shall force to give up their free kingdom of
the air and go into a prison pot under the
watch and ward of a practiced cook. My Lord
Katie greets you with respectful friendship,
but the worse for you, for vice versa, if my
wife salutes you, I salute yours, tit for tat.—[18]

Is there not "ein hurtiger und frölicher Geselle" that is expressing itself in the above
letter?[19]

It is of interest to the psychologist to note
that the humor-element in Luther's personality is often associated with the cruel side of
his personality.[20] In his invectives against
Dr. Eck, he calls him Dr. Geck, meaning "dude,"
or even Dr. Dreck, meaning "dirt". Dr. Usingen
becomes in Luther's wrath Dr. Unsinn, which

is the German for "nonsense". Dr. Crotus becomes Doktor Kröt, which is the German for
"toad" or "ugly wretch."[21] At any rate, it is to be
noted that the lighter vein in Luther's personality tends to excesses. One cannot help but
feeling the sacrilegeous in the playful utterances at times on religious references.[22]

But, as remarked, back of all his humor lay
a deep shadow which acted as a refiner and as
a check, and which played the role of counter-
part, a cross-current to this trait. We do not
have to seek it, for "melancholy" is that shadow
appearing and re-appearing throughout the
course of his life of struggle.

> I know a man who has often, though only
> for brief periods, suffered the pains of hell
> such as no tongue or pen could describe and
> no one could believe, if he had not himself
> felt them. If they had lasted for a half or even
> a tenth part of an hour, he would have per-
> ished altogether and his bones would have
> crumbled to ashes.[23]

> I received your last letters of condolence,
> my dear Gerard (Wilskamp at Herford) with
> great joy and gratitude: may Christ repay
> you. It is true that this trial is the worst I
> have ever had, and though I have had simi-
> lar experiences ever since my youth, I had
> not expected that it would become so much
> worse now. So far Christ has triumphed, but
> He holds me by a very slender thread.—[24]

—I was for more than a whole week in
death and hell (illness in 1527 and the spiritual depression which accompanied it), so
that I was sick all over, and my limbs still
tremble. I almost lost Christ in the waves
and blasts of despair and blasphemy against
God, but God was moved by the prayers of
saints and began to take pity on me and rescue my soul from the lowest hell. Do not
cease to pray for me as I for you, for I believe that even my agony is for others.—We
who are Christ's, despised little flock that
we are, have to suffer the public hatred of
the world and evils enough of our own, to
say nothing of poverty and other humilia-
tions.—Farewell, with all that are yours and
ours, and have us in your prayers, as dead
men who live, as captives who are free, as
sufferers who are safe. May Christ, the con-
queror of death, of hell, of sin, of the world
and the flesh, be and grow in us and you
by His Spirit. Amen.

M. L.[25]

—Thank you, dear Agricola, for the comfort you have given me in writing that your
church is anxious about me and prays for
me. —Please do not stop comforting me and
praying for me, because I am poor and needy.
—*Satan himself rages with his whole might
within me* and the Lord has put me in his
power like another Job. The devil tempts me
with great infirmity of spirit, but through
the prayers of the saints I am not left altogether in his hands, although the wounds he
gives my heart will be hard to heal. I hope

that my trial will profit many, although there is no punishment that my own sins do not deserve.—Truly—I suffer more in spirit from the attacks of the prince of this world himself. In all things blessed be God and the Father of our Lord Jesus Christ, who accomplishes His holy, good and pleasing will in me, but O God! how unsearchably! Amen.[26]

—Pray for me, wretched and despised worm that I am, vexed with a spirit of sadness by the good will of the Father of mercies, to Whom be glory even in my wretchedness. —I seek for nothing else and thirst for nothing else than a gracious God—I who am Christ's sick man. —Does God afflict me with all his floods?[27]

—Do you pray for us. —For many months now I have been suffering from restlessness and faintheartedness; it is Christ's will; pray for me that my faith fail not.—Bugenhagen is living with me now, not so much for his own sake as rather for mine, so that he can keep me company in my loneliness. My Katie, too, greets you—.[28]

—I thank you, dear Jonas, for your prayers and occasional letters. —Judases (referring to Erasmus, the sacramentarians, Zwingli?) as they are they do well to stamp on my wretched self, making me feel as did Christ when He said: "He persecuted the poor and needy man, that He might even slay the broken in heart." I bear God's wrath because I have sinned against Him. Pope, Emperor, princes, bishops, and the whole world hate and persecute me, nor is this enough, but my brothers, too, must add to my sorrows, and my sins and death and Satan, with his angels rage without ceasing. What could save and console me if Christ, too, should desert me, on Whose account they all hate me? But He will not leave the poor sinner at the end, though I believe that I am the least of all men. *Would that Erasmus and the sacramentarians might feel the anguish of my heart for a quarter of an hour*—but now my enemies are strong and live and add grief to my grief, and whom the Lord hath smitten they persecute. But enough of this, or I may be a complainer, impatient of the rod of God, who smites and heals, kills and makes alive, Who is blessed in His holy and perfect will. It must be that one whom the world and its prince thus hate is pleasing to Christ.—Behold the wickedness of Satan and of men! We Wittenbergers are the hatred and the disgust and the fear of all men; as says the Psalm (22, 6), "A reproach of men and despised of the people," but we are, as we hope, the joy and crown of angels and saints. Amen.

MARTIN LUTHER, Christi lutum
(Christ's mud)[29]

—By God's mercy I am alive and am well enough in body, but what I am or what I do in spirit, I scarcely know myself. What the world does—the Pope, the Emperor, the Kings—I care little. I sigh for Christ and His grace unto salvation.—Satan is busy and wants to keep me from writing anything more, but rather to take me with him down to hell; may Christ trample him under foot. Amen—[30]

—About ten years ago I first felt *this despair* and fear of divine wrath. Afterwards I obtained rest when I married and had good days, but *later it returned.* When I complained to Staupitz he said he had never felt such trials, "but as far as I can see" he said, "they are more necessary to us than food and drink." Who feel such temptations should accustom themselves to bearing them, for so doing is real Christianity. If Satan had not tried me thus I could not hate him so much, nor do him so much harm, so that my trials seem to me gifts of God—.[31]

—At the end of my letter I beg you to pray the Lord for me, for I confess to you that *my life approaches nearer hell, for I become worse and more miserable all the time.* Farewell.

An exiled son of Adam,
MARTIN LUTHER, Augustinian[32]

—So much for others, now about myself. What will you—I pray you praise the Lord even in a sinner like me. *I hate my wretched life; I fear death; I am empty of faith* and full of qualities which, Christ knows, I should much prefer to do without, were it not to serve him thereby.[33]

—Though I am well, I am compelled to be a sick man almost all the time, for Satan is harassing me, and that keeps me from writing and doing other things, for I must seek society so that I may not run the risk of solitude. Do you pray for me—.[34]

(Gal. II:20 "For me") Who is this me? Even
I, wretched and damnable sinner, so dearly
beloved of the Son of God, that he gave himself for me.—Dost thou not hear, O thou
wretch, that the Son of God shed his blood
for thee?—If I, being a wretch and a damned
sinner, could be redeemed by another price,
what needed the Son of God to be given for
me?—For he delivered neither sheep, ox,
gold, nor silver, but even God himself,
entirely and wholly, "for me" even for "me,"
I say, a miserable and wretched sinner.
Now therefore in that the Son of God was
thus delivered to death for me, I take comfort and apply this unto myself.—For I myself, even in this great light of the Gospel,
wherein I have been so long exercised,
have much ado to hold this definition of
Christ which Paul here giveth; so deeply
hath the doctrine and pestilent opinion that
Christ is a lawgiver, entered even as it were
oil in my bones. Ye young men, therefore,
are in this case more happy than we that
are old. For ye are not infected with these
pernicious errors, wherein I have been so
nustled and so drowned *even from my youth,*
that at the very hearing of the name of
Christ my heart trembled and quaked for
fear; for I was persuaded that he was a severe
judge. Wherefore it is to me a double travail
and trouble to correct and reform this evil;
first, to forget, to condemn, and to resist
this old grounded error, that Christ is a
lawgiver and a judge; *for it always return-
eth and plucketh me back:* then to plant in

my heart a new and true persuasion of Christ that he is a justifier and a Saviour. Ye, I say, that are young, may learn with much less difficulty, to know Christ purely and sincerely, if ye will. Wherefore if any man feel himself oppressed with heaviness and anguish of heart, he must not impute it unto Christ—but unto the devil.—What could be said, I pray you, more sweet and comfortable to the poor afflicted conscience?[35]

Such epistles and extracts as these, taken from various years of the Reformer's life, speak in no uncertain terms of this melancholic trait which brought the man, ofttimes, into the pit of despair. He was of a tender conscience. The self-abnegative and the melancholic are related strains; the warm-hearted, the affectionate and the tender, also. Veit Dietrich wrote, for example, of Luther mourning bitterly of the death of his father: "He took his Psalter and went to his room and wept so much that for two days he couldn't work."[36]

His melancholy brought him into the very bottom of the pit of despair. Few have suffered such an affliction of this trait as he. While at Wartburg, he wrote Melanchthon:

I congratulate Dr. Lupine on his happy death. Would that we too might live no longer! The wrath of God, which in my leisure I am daily observing more and more, is such that I doubt whether He will save anybody except infants from this kingdom of Satan. *Our God has so deserted us!*[37]

The melancholic in him is not to be wondered at, when we acquaint ourselves with the fact that he was a constant prey to torturing diseases. He speaks of his nervous troubles, accompanied with dizziness, a ringing in the ears, and sleeplessness; of his frequent and severe attacks of indigestion, of gout, rheumatism, sciatica, his sufferings brought on with ulcers, abscesses in the ears, tooth-ache, stone (disease of the kidney and bladder) and the palpitation of the heart, etc. In the light of all this extreme suffering, it is remarkable to witness the constant good spirits, humor and jocoseness, on the other hand, which played such a significant role in his personality and which led his companions to say of the melancholic Father Martin that he was "von Natur ein hurtiger und frölicher Geselle." Professor J. M. Reu remarks: "Thus does the greatness of his genius only show itself all the more resplendent when we think of his numerous illnesses".[38]

Truly, the "humor" and the "melancholy" are in him marked cross-currents which did much to mold his personality and his life's work!

Section 4.   Practical-Temper—Mysticism

By "practical-temper" we would mean that peculiar magnanimity in Luther which is seen in the wide and multifarious interests which claimed his attention, and to which he responded as well. He was a practical, an active soul; a hard-headed organizer. He was a profound student, not of the recluse type but one who had the gift to impart, adapt, and apply the results of his studies to the needs of the world outside. One stands in amazement before his capacity and ability to meet complicated and unprecedented problems, to handle and direct the machinery of a rising cause and widely spreading organization. One stands in bewilderment before his versatility of interests, ranging from a business manager of a fish-farm (as he called it) to one of the world's greatest composers of hymnology. One wonders how it was possible that he could contribute to so many fields of so many ranges,—contributions which call forth the gratitude of later and succeeding generations.

He was a man of action; a keen observer even to slight details. He was an outstanding University Professor, perhaps one of the greatest of the world's pulpit-men, besides a level-headed administrator. He was an author with a prolific pen, the products of which, as he once remarked, kept three presses going all the time. He complained often that the printers were lazy, inasmuch as they did not keep up with him. "It was his habit to send copy to the printer day by day, and he was nearly always reading the proof of the earlier pages of a book while writing the later. Often the preface was in type before the work itself was even begun."[1] A complete edition of Luther's writings would to-day fill more than one hundred good size volumes.[2] "Despite his public labors," writes Professor McGiffert, "which continued unabated, Luther showed himself no little of a family man. He did considerable gardening, and took a great interest in getting rare plants from distant parts of the country. Not long after his marriage he wrote Spalatin: "I have planted a garden and dug a well, and both have turned out successfully. Come, and you shall be crowned with lilies and roses." He provided himself with a carpenter's bench and a turning-lathe, securing through his friend Link in Nuremberg the best tools to be had, and he proved not unskillful in making useful articles for the house. He continued to mend his own clothes, not, as he declared, for the sake of economy, but because the tailors were so poor. On one occasion, Käthe had to complain, he cut up one of the children's garments to patch his own trousers with."[3]

Better than to enumerate his interests with their practical significances, would be to glean extracts from his own pen where we may catch the spirit of this trait. Great variety of interests, and a mind responding with practical advice and suggestions!

—To the question whether a prince (Duke John Frederick of Saxony) can allow the taking of usurious interest, I reply: It would be a fine thing if tithes of all property were paid to the government every year, as

was the custom in the ancient world. That
would be the kind of interest most in accordance with God's will.—if God gave much
or little the tithe would be reckoned accord-
ingly.—I must—say that it is highly necessary that the taking of interest should be
regulated everywhere, but to abolish it
entirely would not be right either, for it
can be made just.—In saying this I am
speaking only of the interest which does
not exceed four or five per cent.—But if the
rate exceeds five percent, every prince
should take measures to reduce it to four
or five percent and to secure some reduction
of the capital proportioned to the length of
time it has been invested. This should be
done mildly, so that it might be a beginning
toward regulating the whole business and
bringing it, in the course of time, to a just
basis.—[4]

—I am compelled to ask your help, Jerome,
with the many poor. The youth who brings
this letter to you, one Gregory Keser, is
looking for work, and asked me for an in-
troduction to some citizen of Nuremberg.—
If you want your Katie von Bora, you had
best act quickly, before she is given to some
one else who wants her. She has not yet conquered her love for you. I would gladly see
you married to each other—.[5]

—I do not think it well to hold a council
of our party for the purpose of establishing
unity in ceremonies. It would set a bad example, however zealous and well-meant the
effort were, as all the councils of the Church,

from the very beginning, prove. Even the
Apostolic Council dealt almost more with
works and traditions than with faith, but in
the later councils there was no discussion
of faith, but always of opinions and ques-
tions so that the very word "council" is to
me almost as suspicious and distasteful as
the word "free-will." If one church does not
wish to imitate another in these external
things, why should it be compelled to do so
by decrees of councils which are soon con-
verted into laws and snares for souls? Let
one church, therefore, imitate another of its
own accord, or else let it be allowed to use
its own customs.—[6]

—Your grace allowed us this year to have
some wheat from the collector, and now the
collector duns us every day, and we cannot
pay for it, because we are not getting and
have not been getting our revenues. I therefore humbly petition your Grace to excuse
us for the last time from paying the said
collector for this wheat, for I believe and
hope that it will not be necessary any more.

—But in order that we, who are the last inmates, may not go away entirely empty-
handed, I humbly ask that your Grace will
graciously grant and convey either to the
prior or to me in my own name, the plot ad-
joining the hospital which our monastery
bought for N. gulden. Not that I wish to have
from your Grace a public grant or deed, for
I know very well how much importance
your Grace attaches to that; but I wish your
Grace to wink at it, so that we may take pos-

session with a clear conscience, and by a secret grant. Thus we could use my name to resist or defend ourselves against anyone who wanted to be grasping or otherwise too shrewd, and then appeal to your Grace as though petitioning for a grant and permit yet to be issued.—[7]

Grace and peace. I return the Mass. I am willing that it should be sung as you have indicated, but it does not altogether please me that Latin music has been kept for German words. I have told the publisher what German melody I should like to have put there. The catechism has been assigned to the men who are to write it, as I said before. I owe a book on the freedom of the will, but I am so overwhelmed by the demands of the printers that I am compelled to put it off. I wish the "Preface" to be very short. If you cannot compose a better one, you may use meanwhile the one outlined on the enclosed sheet.—[8]

Luther to the City Council of Danzig.

Grace and peace.—On your written request I did my best to get you a proper preacher. It was not possible to give you John Bugenhagen, whom you mentioned as the man you wished to have, for our church here was not willing to let him go, since we must keep men here by whom we can train other men and so serve other cities too. Therefore I am sending you Master Michael Hänlein, who is in all respects a pious and prudent and well-mannered man.—I commend him to you in the hope that you will receive him

well—and will see to it that he is provided
for in a Christian and proper manner.—

And see to it that no fanatics come among
you.—If anything—images or anything else
—is to be changed or destroyed it ought not
to be done by the people but by the regular
authority of the city council, so that the bad
practice of despising the authorities does
not get a foothold among you, as it has elsewhere: for it is the will of God that they shall
be feared and honored.—[9]

I have written your Grace's father and
lord, my gracious Lord, that he shall set the
university in order and secure a man who
will undertake the task. It is true that your
Grace has much else to do in these troublous
times, but in this matter, too, delay is dangerous, for things have been hanging in the air
long enough, and everything is upset. Besides, men are moving away and being called
away every day.—Necessity, therefore, demands that if we are to continue to have a
university here, we must take prompt action. It were a pity if such a school from
which the Gospel has gone out into all the
world, were to go down, and if, when men are
needed everywhere, nothing were done to
educate them.—For your Grace sees that the
world cannot now be ruled by force alone,
but must have men of learning.—If there were
no preachers and teachers the temporal
government would not long endure—.[10]

—In the first place your Grace will pardon
me for having been so insistent upon the
reorganization of the university.—Therefore, gracious Lord, now that the university

is set in order, and the Order of Worship has
been composed and is about to go into use,
there remain two things which demand the
attention and disposition of your Grace, as
our temporal Lord. The first thing is that
the parishes everywhere are in such miserable condition. No one gives anything or
pays for anything: the mass fees are
abolished and either there are no taxes at
all, or else they are too small; the common
man does not think of the priests and preachers, and unless your Grace makes a strict
law and undertakes to give proper support
to the parishes and preaching places, there
will soon be no parsonages or schools or
pupils.—There are enough monasteries,
foundations, benefices, charitable endow-
ments and the like if only your Grace will
interest himself sufficiently to command
that they be inspected, reckoned up and
organized.—

The second thing is a matter of which I
once spoke with your Grace here at Wittenberg.
Your Grace ought to order an inspection of
the temporal government also, and ascer-
tain how the city councils and all other officials conduct their government and preside
over the common weal. For there is great
complaint on all sides of bad government,
both in the cities and in the country, and it
is your Grace's duty, as the ruler of the land,
to look into it. Perhaps the petitions and
appeals and complaints to the court would
become fewer, if the state were to institute
such an inspection and some good regula-
tion—.[11]

Luther to the Elector John of Saxony
November 30, 1525

God's grace and peace in Christ. Highborn Prince, gracious Lord. Your Grace has replied to my suggestion that the parishes generally be investigated. It is not my idea, that all the pastors should be paid out of your Grace's treasury, but because your Grace graciously asks my judgment about how the matter shall be undertaken, I give it as my humble opinion that your Grace should cause all the parishes in the principality to be inspected, and if it is found that the people desire evangelical preachers and the parish funds are insufficient for their support then your Grace should command that the community must pay a certain sum annually, either through the town council or otherwise. For if they desire pastors, it is your Grace's office to hold them to the duty of rewarding the laborers, as the Gospel commands.

Such a visitation might be conducted in this way. Your Grace might divide his dominions into four or five parts and send into each part two men chosen from the nobles, perhaps, or the officials, who would inform themselves about these parishes and their income, and learn what the pastor needs, and then lay upon the parishes your Grace's command regarding the annual tax. But if the expense or the trouble of this procedure were too great for your Grace, citizens from the towns could be used for this purpose, or representatives of the chief towns of the district could be summoned and the matter discussed with them. Whatever best pleases your Grace, let that be done.

Moreover, care must be taken concerning the old pastors or those otherwise unfit for office. If they are good men in other respects and not opposed to the Gospel they ought to be obligated to read the Gospels and the Postils.—Thus the people would receive a true ministration of the Gospel in return for the support they gave the pastor. It would not be a good thing to put the men out of office they have been holding without some recompense, if only they are not opposed to the Gospel.—[12]

> Luther to John Agricola
> Wittenberg July 1527

Grace and peace. I have gladly and willingly received your Elsa, my dear Agricola. Her illness is, as you see, rather of the mind than of the body. I am comforting her as much as I can, with my knowledge. You could have done the same thing, except that woman in such a case believes anybody else sooner than her own husband.—In a word, her disease is not for the apothecaries (as they call them), nor is it to be treated with the salves of Hippocrates, but by constantly applying plasters of Scripture and the Word of God. For what has conscience to do with Hippocrates? Therefore, I would dissuade you from the use of medicine and advise the power of God's Word.—[13]

Luther to the Margrave George of Brandenburg

July 18, 1529

—In the first place, we think it well that the monasteries and foundations should be left as they are until they die out, for so long as the old inmates still live there is little hope that there will be any peace if they are forced either to introduce or put up with such innovations.—But whatever of the old, good order of worship it is desired to reintroduce is best put into the schools and the parish churches where the common man too, can be present and be touched by it, etc., as we do here in Wittenberg and in other cities.

In the second place, it would be good if in your Grace's principality your Grace would establish one or two universities, where not only the Holy Scriptures, but law and all the sciences would be taught. From these schools learned men could be got as preachers, pastors, secretaries, councilors, etc., for the whole principality. To this purpose the income of the monasteries and foundations could be applied so that scholars could be maintained in the schools at proper salaries, viz., two theologians, two jurists, one professor of medicine, one mathematician, and for logic, rhetoric, etc., four or five men.

For, if studying is to be good you must have not empty cloisters and deserted monasteries and endowed churches, but a city, in which many people come together and practice on one another and stir each other up and drive each other on. Solitary studies do not accomplish this, but common studies do, for when many are together one gives another incentive and example.

In the third place, it is well that in all towns and villages good primary schools should be established out of which could be picked and chosen those who were fit for the universities, out of which the men can then be taken who are to serve your land and people. If the towns or their citizens cannot do this, then it would be well to establish new stipends for the support of a few bright fellows in the deserted monasteries, so that every town might have one or two students.—[14]

A preacher should be a logician and a rhetorician, that is, he must be able to teach, and to admonish; when he preaches touching an article, he must, first, distinguish it. Secondly, he must define, describe, and show what it is. Thirdly, he must produce sentences out of the Scriptures, therewith to prove and strengthen it. Fourthly, he must, with examples, explain and declare it. Fifthly, he must adorn it with similitudes; and, lastly, he must admonish and rouse up the lazy, earnestly reprove all the disobedient, all false doctrine, and the authors thereof; yet, not out of malice and envy, but only to God's honor, and the profit and saving health of the people.[15]

Divinity consists in use and practice, not in speculation and meditation. Every one that deals in speculations, either in household affairs or temporal government, without practice, is lost and nothing worth. When a tradesman makes his account, how much profit he shall reap in the year, but puts nothing in practice, he trades in vain speculations, and finds afterwards that his reckoning comes far too short. And thus it goes also with speculating divines, as is seen to this day, and as I know by experience.[16]

A good preacher should have these properties and virtues; first, to teach systematically; secondly, he should have a ready wit; thirdly, he should be eloquent; fourthly, he should have a good voice; fifthly, a good memory; sixthly, he should know when to make an end; seventhly, he should be sure of his doctrine; eighthly, he should venture and engage body and blood, wealth and honor, in the Word; ninthly, he should suffer himself to be mocked and jeered of every one.[17]

It is not possible to reproduce a foreign idiom in one's native tongue. The proper method of translation is to seek a vocabulary neither too free nor too literal, but to select the most fitting terms according to the usage of the language adopted.
To translate properly is to render the spirit of a foreign language into our own idiom. I do this with such care in translating Moses that the Jews accuse me of rendering only the sense and not the precise words. For example, when the Hebrew says, "the mouth of the sword" I translate "the edge of the sword," though in this case it

might be objected that the word "mouth" is a figurative allusion to preachers who destroy by word of mouth.

I try to speak as men do in the market-place. Didactic, philosophic, and sententious books are, therefore, hard to translate, but narrative easy. In rendering Moses I make him so German that no one would know that he was a Jew.[18]

Now by God's grace it has come to pass that children may learn with pleasure, be it a language or some other art or science or history. Our schools are no more the hell and purgatory in which we were martyred by declension and conjugation, although we learned nothing of value with all our whipping, trembling, anguish and crying. If people now take so much time teaching their children to play cards and dance, why should they not take an equal amount to teach them to read and learn other things while they are young, idle, and curious? For my part, if I had children they would have to learn not only the languages and history but also singing, music, and the whole mathematics.—It is a sorrow to me that I was not taught to read more poetry and history.[19]

The Italian painters are so able and so full of genius that they can, in a masterly way, follow and exactly imitate nature in all their paintings; not only do they get the proper color and form in all the members, but they even make them appear as if they lived and moved. Flanders follows Italy and imitates her in some measure, for the men of the Low Countries, especially the Flemish, are cunning and artful; they quickly and easily learn a foreign language, for they have ready tongues.[20]

Dances are instituted that courtesy may be learned in company and friendship and acquaintance be contracted between young men and girls. Here their intercourse may be watched and occasion of honorable meeting given, so that having tried a girl we can afterwards let her go about more safely and easily. The Pope formerly condemned dances because he was an enemy of marriage. But let all things be done decently! Let honorable men and nations be invited to see that everything is proper. I myself would attend them sometimes, but the youth would whirl less giddily if I did.[21]

An Open Letter to the Christian Nobility
Of the German Nation
Concerning
The Reform of the Christian Estate
1520

———

III. Proposals For Reform

Now, although I am too small a man to make propositions which might effect a reform in this dreadful state of things, nevertheless I may as well sing my fool's song to the end, and say, as far as I am able, what could and should be done by the temporal authorities or by a general council.

1. Every prince, nobleman and city should boldly forbid their subjects to pay the annates to Rome and should abolish them entirely—.

2.—They should ordain, order, and decree, that henceforth no benefice shall be drawn into the hands of Rome—.

3. An imperial law should be issued, that no bishop's cloak and no confirmation of any dignity whatsoever shall henceforth be secured from Rome—.

4. It should be decreed that no temporal matter shall be taken to Rome, but that all such cases shall be left to the temporal authorities—.

5. No more reservations should be valid, and no more benefices should be seized by Rome—.

6. The casus reservati, the "reserved cases" (legal actions which could only be heard in Rome), should be abolished—.

7. The Roman See should also do away with the officia, and diminish the swarm of vermin at Rome, so that the pope's household can be supported by the pope's own purse—.

8. The hard and terrible oaths should be abolished, which the bishops are wrongfully compelled to render to the pope—.

9. The pope should have no authority over the emperor, except that he anoints and crowns him at the altar, just as a bishop anoints and crowns a king—.

10. The pope should restrain himself, take his fingers out of the pie, and claim

not title to the kingdom of Naples and Sicily—.

11. The kissing of the pope's feet should take place no more. It is an unchristian, nay, an antichristian thing for a poor sinful man to let his feet be kissed by one who is a hundred times better than himself—.

12. Pilgrimages to Rome should either be abolished, or else no one should be allowed to make such a pilgrimage out of curiosity or because of a pious impulse, unless it is first recognized by his parishpriest, his town authorities or his overlord, that he has good and sufficient reason for it—.

13. Next we come to that crowd who vow much and keep little.—The building of mendicant houses should no more be permitted.—The mendicants should also be relieved of preaching.—The pope must also be forbidden to found and confirm any more of these orders—.

14.—Every city should have a priest or bishop, as St. Paul clearly says in Titus I; and this priest should not be compelled to live without a wedded wife.—My advice is that matrimony be again made free, and that every one be left free choice to marry or not to marry—.

15. Nor must I forget the poor convents!— I advise these children, brethren and sisters: If your superiors are unwilling to grant you permission to confess your secret sins to whomsoever you wish, then take them to whatever brother or sister you will and con-

fess them, receive absolution, and then go and do whatever you wish and ought to do—.

16. It were also necessary to abolish all anniversary, mortuary and "soul" masses, or at least to diminish their number—.

17. Certain of the penalties or punishments of the canon law should also be abolished, especially the interdict—.

18. All festivals should be abolished, and Sunday alone retained—.

19. The grades or degrees within which marriage is forbidden should be changed.— This is the place to say too that the fasts should be matters of liberty, and all sorts of food made free—.

20. The forest chapels and rustic churches must be utterly destroyed (i.e. churches which are built in the country, where there are no congregations)—.

21. One of our greatest necessities is the abolition of all begging throughout Christendom.—Every city could support its own poor.—In my judgment there is no other business in which so much knavery and deceit are practiced as in begging—.

22. It is also to be feared that the many masses which are endowed in the foundations and monasteries are not only of little use, but greatly arouse the wrath of God.— Again, no one person should be allowed any longer to hold more than one canonry or prebend. He must be content with a modest position, that some one else may also have something—.

23. Sodalities, indulgences, letters of in-

dulgence, "butter-letters", mass-letters, dispensations, and everything else of the sort, are to be drowned and destroyed. There is nothing good in them.—

24. It is high time that we seriously and honestly consider the case of the Bohemians, and come into union with them so that the terrible slander, hatred and envy on both sides may cease. (Bohemians, i.e. the Hussites).—We must honestly confess the truth—and grant the Bohemians that John Hus and Jerome of Prague were burned at Constance in violation of the papal, Christian, imperial safe-conduct and oath.—If I knew that the Picards (the Bohemian Brethren) held no other error touching the sacrament of the altar except that they believe that the bread and wine are present in their true nature, but that the body and blood of Christ are truly present under them, then I would not condemn them—.

25. The Universities also need a good, thorough reformation.—In this regard my advice would be that Aristotle's "Physics," "Metaphysics," "On the Soul," "Ethics," which have hitherto been thought his best books, should be altogether discarded.—I should be glad to see Aristotle's books on "Logic," "Rhetoric" and "Poetics" retained or used in an abridged form.—The medical men I leave to reform their own faculties, the jurists and theologians—I say—that it were well if the canon law, from the first letter to the last, and especially the decretals, were utterly blotted out.—The number

of theological books must also be lessened, and a selection made of the best of them.— Above all, the foremost and most general subject of study, both in the higher and the lower schools, should be the Holy Scriptures and for the young boys the Gospel. And would to God that every town had a girls' school also—.

26. I know full well that the Roman crowd will make pretentions and great boasts about how the pope took the Holy Roman Empire from the Greek Emperor and bestowed it on the Germans, for which honor and benevolence he is said to have justly deserved and obtained from the Germans submission and thanks—let the German Emperor be really and truly emperor—.

27.—There is great need of a general law and decree of the German nation against the extravagances and excess in dress.—

—In like manner it is also necessary to restrict the spice-traffic.

—But the greatest misfortune of the German nation is certainly the traffic in annuities.

—Next comes the abuse of eating and drinking which gives us Germans a bad reputation in foreign lands, as though it were a special vice.

—Finally, is it not a pitiful thing that we Christians should maintain among us open and common houses of prostitution, though all of us are baptized unto chastity?

Wittenberg, 1520.[22]

If we should characterize the general impression given by such passages as above, we would find no better and more inclusive description of the man behind such utterances than "a wide-awake leader and reformer of *practical-temper.*" A review of Luther's sermons would give us the same impression, a prophet, indeed, fully aware of existing conditions, pointing out the prevailing sins and suggesting practical remedies to reformation. Wide-awake, alert to his environment together with a keen sense of responsibility which threw him headlong into conflict. Yet, again, there appears in him a striking opposite current which makes us wonder, in reading many of his passages whether, indeed, there is not another man behind the utterances. Mysticism and practical-mindedness are indeed opposites. The former is characterized by a high degree of subjective-mindedness with the tendency to withdraw from the open-field of conflict to the inner-field of more pressing problems, while the latter is characterized by a high-degree of objective-mindedness with the tendency to action and combat with situations and with other persons. The above extracts from Luther's pen plainly reveal his objective-mindedness: his "practical-temper."

Yet the mystic in him, the subjective-mindedness in him is even as strong; we find in him a constant tendency to return to himself and his own inner and self-consciousness with its conflicts, which gave birth to the mystic utterances of a self-reflective soul. Mystics are seldom of a practical-temper. Men of practical-temper are seldom mystics. Each can hardly understand the ways and the expressions of the other. Religion historically, has found itself divided into these two camps and perhaps always will, those who are concerned with the problems of their own salvation and who are prone to live in "other-worldliness," and those who emphasize the ethical and the social expressions of man in his relation with other men in the present world-environment as constituting the heart and essence of that which goes under the name of Religion.

In Luther, the practical and the mystical have a happy combination, both with strong tendencies to expression. At times, the practical-temper of his mind overshadowed any of the mysticism in him.[23] At times, again, the subjective side, the mystical, overshadows the practical and objective interests to such an extent as to give him a place as one of the outstanding of the greater religious mystics. Each trait acted as a check to excess on the other. Yet, each is a "real presence" in the make up of his personality.

His fervent prayer at Worms is certainly the prayer of a mystic who is enwrapped in the agonies of a troubled spirit, his cries to God are surely the characteristic cries of the mystic who longs to be at-one with the Higher Power:

Almighty and Eternal God, how is there but one thing to be seen upon earth! How the people open wide their mouths! How small and insignificant is their trust in God! How tender and weak the flesh, and how mighty and active the devil.—If I should turn my eyes in that direction, it would be all over with me; the clock would strike the hour, and sentence would be passed. O God! O God! O Thou, my God! Do Thou, my God, stand by me, against all the world's wisdom and reason. Oh, do it! Thou must do it! Yea, Thou alone must do it! Not mine, but Thine, is the cause. For my own self, I have nothing to do with these great earthly lords. I would prefer to have peaceful days, and to be out of this turmoil. But Thine, O Lord, is this cause; it is righteous and eternal. Stand by me, Thou true Eternal God! In no man do I trust. All that is of the flesh and that savours of the flesh, is here of no account. God, O God! dost Thou not hear me, O my God? Art Thou dead? No. Thou canst not die; Thou art only hiding Thyself. Hast Thou chosen me for this work? I ask Thee how I may be sure of this, if it be Thy will; for I would never have taught, in all my life, of undertaking aught against such great lords. Stand by me, O God, in the Name of Thy dear Son, Jesus Christ, who shall be my Defender and Shelter, yea, my Mighty Fortress, through the might and strength of Thy Holy Ghost. Lord, where abidest Thou? Thou art my God; where art Thou? Come! come! I am ready to lay down my life patiently as

a lamb. For the cause is right and it is Thine,
so shall I never be separated from Thee. Let
all be done in Thy Name!—the soul is Thine,
and belongs to Thee, and shall abide with
Thee eternally. Amen. God help me. Amen.[24]

This cry from the deep for union with his
Lord rises to the heights of its answer with a
tremendous sense of security, peace, and personal one-ness in Luther's famous hymn: "Ein
feste Burg ist unser Gott." It is the expression
of one who has through a deep mystical experience, sought and found peace, assurance,
and strength in the inner-recesses of an otherwise turbulent soul. All obstacles are overcome. Victory is surely his. He is on God's
side, the cause is His. The world with its mighti-
est opposition fades before a new-born experience and conviction that God and Victory are
imminent:

> Ein feste Burg ist unser Gott,
> Ein gute Wehr und Waffen.
> Er hilft uns frei aus aller Noth,
> Die uns jetzt hat betroffen.
> Der alt bose Feind
> Mit Ernst ers jetzt meint,
> Gross Macht und viel List
> Sein grausam Rustung ist,
> Auf Erd ist nicht seins Gleichen.
>
> Mit unsrer Macht ist nichts gethan,
> Wir sind gar bald verloren:
> Es streit't fur uns der rechte Mann,
> Den Gott hat selbst erkoren.

Fragst du, wer der ist?
Er heist Jesus Christ,
Der Herr Zebaoth,
Und ist kein andrer Gott.
Das Feld muss er behalten.

Und wenn die Welt voll Teufel war,
Und wollt uns gar verschlingen,
So furchten wir uns nicht so sehr,
Es soll uns doch gelingen.
Der Furst dieser Welt,
Wie sauer er sich stellt,
Thut er uns doch nicht,
Das macht, er ist gerich't.
Ein Wörtlein kann ihn fällen.

Das Wort sie sollen lassen stahn,
Und kein Dank dazu haben,
Er ist bei uns wol auf dem Plan
Mit seinem Geist und Gaben.
Nehmen sie den Leib,
Gut, Ehr, Kind und Weib,
Lass fahren dahin,
Sie habens kein Gewinn,
Das Reich muss uns doch bleiben.[25]

The mysticism of St. Paul which seems to have expressed itself frequently in a feeling of self-absorption with an accompanying sense of quietism, is similarly experienced by Luther as he himself expressed in commenting on St. Paul's Letter to the Galatians 2:20 ("I am crucified with Christ: nevertheless I live; yet not I, but Christ liveth in me: and the life which I now live in the flesh I live by the faith of the Son of God, who loved me, and gave himself for me"):[26]

He is my form, my furniture, and perfec-
tion, adorning and beautifying my faith, as
the colour, the clear light, or the whiteness,
do garnish and beautify the wall. Thus are
we constrained grossly to set forth this matter. For we cannot spiritually conceive,
that Christ is so nearly joined and united
unto us, as the colour or whiteness is unto
the wall. Christ, therefore, saith he, thus
joined and united unto me, and abiding in
me, liveth this life in me which now I live:
yea, Christ himself, is this life which now
I live. Wherefore Christ and I in this behalf
are both one.[27]

This is no mere commentary with Luther, but
a confession. He was blessed with this feeling
of complete unity with the divine in his religious
experiences which made him feel so akin to
the experiences and expressions of the Apostle
Paul. Let it not be understood that these mystical experiences were uniformly present
with him; had they been so, we would not be
considering the "cross-currents" in him. But
that he had typical mystical experiences is
evident throughout his writings.

It is noteworthy that he finds an affinity with
the great German mystic Tauler (died 1361), as
he himself admitted to Spalatin in 1516:

—I will add a piece of advice. If you de-
light in reading pure, sound theology, like
that of the earliest age, and in German, read
the sermons of John Tauler, the Dominican,
of which I send you, as it were, the quintes-
sence. I have never read either in Latin or

in our own tongue theology more wholesome
or more agreeable to the gospel. Taste and
see, therefore, *how sweet is the Lord,* as you
have first tasted and seen how bitter is
everything in us.—[28]

William James quotes the following instance
and confession of Luther as revealing a typical mystical temper and mystical suscepti-
bility: "'When a fellow monk,'" said Luther,
"'one day repeated the words of the Creed:
(I believe in the forgiveness of sins), I saw the
Scripture in an entirely new light; and straight-
way I felt as if I were born anew. It was as if I
had found the door of paradise thrown wide
open.'"[29]

Quiet hours of prayer and devotion continued
throughout his life as the main-spring to his
strength and courage. His saying, "Oratio,
Tentatio, Meditatio faciunt Theologum" is now
famous. Developing the idea of "Oratio," he
said:

> Kneel in thy closet, and with real humility
> and earnestness beg God that through His
> dear Son He will give His Holy Spirit to you
> to enlighten you, guide you, and give you
> understanding, as thou seest that David in
> the 119th Psalm continually begs: "Teach
> me, Lord; show me; guide me; instruct me,"
> and the like. Even though he had the text
> of Moses, and well knew other books and
> daily heard and read them, yet did he wish
> to have the real Master of the Scripture also

that he might not be left to his own reason
and be his own teacher.[30]

How tender, and how deep his religious and
mystical experiences were, is evidenced by
such passages:

> When true contrition is about to arise from
> the goodness and benefits of God, especially
> from the wounds of Christ, so that man
> first comes to (a sense of) his ingratitude
> from the *contemplation* of the divine good-
> ness,—then *tears flow,* and he will heartily
> hate himself, but without despair since he
> will hate his sin, not on account of its penal-
> ty, but on account of his view of the goodness
> of God which, being beheld, preserves him
> that he may not despair and may hate him-
> self ardently, even with delight.[31]

> —God speaks (sonat) and teaches inwardly
> to the heart.—(There is an) inward whisper-
> ing: Thy sins are forgiven thee.[32]

> When thou hearest that he suffered for
> thee, and believest, there springs up al-
> ready confidence toward him and tender
> love, and thus perishes all love of (other)
> things as useless, and there arises a pas-
> sionate *regard for Christ alone as the One
> Thing necessary, and there remains to thee
> nothing save Jesus only,* he alone enough
> and sufficient for thee, so that despairing of
> all things thou hast this Only One, in whom
> thou hopest for all things, and, therefore,
> lovest him above all things. But Jesus is
> the one true and only God whom when thou
> hast, thou hast no strange God.[33]

—I, out of my own experience, am able to witness that Jesus Christ is true God; I know full well and have found what the name of Jesus has done for me. I have often been so near death, that I thought verily now must I die—but always he mercifully put life into me, *refreshed* and comforted me. Therefore, let us use diligence only to keep him, and then all is safe, although the devil were ever so wicked and crafty, and *the world* ever so evil and *false*. Let whatsoever will or can befall me, I will surely cleave by my sweet Saviour Christ Jesus, for in him am I baptized; *I can neither do nor know* anything but only what he has taught me—.[34]

—But I, God be praised, have learned out of the Holy Scripture, and by experience in my trials, temptations and fierce combats against the devil, that this article of Christ's humanity is most sure and certain; for nothing has more or better helped me in high spiritual temptations, than my comfort in this, *that Christ, the true everlasting Son of God, is our flesh and bone,* as St. Paul says to the Ephesians, chapter v "We are members of his body, of his flesh and bone,"—.[35]

Christ once appeared visible here on earth, and showed his glory, and according to the divine purpose of God finished the work of redemption and the deliverance of mankind. I do not desire he should come once more in the same manner, neither would I he should send an angel unto me. Nay, though an angel should come and appear

before mine eyes from heaven, yet it would
not add to my belief; for I have of my Saviour Christ Jesus bond and seal; I have his
Word, Spirit, and sacrament; thereupon I
depend, and desire no new revelations—.[36]

We close this section by setting down a significant remark made by Heine who "was not
disposed by birth or temperament to overesti-
mate the significance of Luther": "Luther is
not only the greatest but the most German man
in our history.—He possessed qualities that
we seldom see associated—nay, that we usually
find in the most hostile antagonism. *He was
at once a dreamy mystic and a practical man
of action.*—He was both a cold scholastic word-
sifter and an inspired God-drunk prophet.—
He was full of the awful reverence of God, full
of self-sacrificing devotion to the Holy Spirit,
*he could lose himself entirely in pure spiri-
tuality.* Yet he was fully acquainted with the
glories of this earth; he knew how estimable
they are.—He was a complete man, I might
say an absolute man, in whom there was no
discord between matter and spirit. To call him
a spiritualist would be as erroneous as to call
him a sensualist—."[37]

Such, indeed, was Luther: a "practical man
of action" and at once a "dreamy mystic." The
cross-currents of the "practical-temper" and
"mysticism" are both strong strains in his
personality.

Section 5. *Critical-Temper—Superstition*

The heading of this section of the two cross-currents in Luther's personality which we shall discuss savors somewhat of the two common divisions made in philosophic attitudes, viz., the critical versus the naive attitudes, or still more common divisions: philosophic versus the pre-philosophic attitudes. At any rate, we feel the distinctions and the opposition of the two attitudes. If, in Luther, we should find him with the naive attitude in the beginning of his career and laid aside later for the critical, there would be nothing unusual, since that is the succession of attitudes of most folk. But, as stated above, we are treating here of "simultaneous" cross-currents, and as such, we feel, that if an individual personality gets expressed now with one and now with another of these attitudes throughout his life, there is in him some discord which is worthy of attention, at least if it is at all marked. Such is the case with Luther. Now, he is critically-minded, compelling the world to humble itself before the severe judgment of his reason, again, he is as naive as a little child acquiescing in the habits, the traditions, the beliefs of his day. The naive in him is especially marked in his superstition. A study of these two conflicting traits is an interesting chapter by itself and affords a unique problem in the psychology of the human personality.

We have already felt the whip of his merciless criticism. Pope, emperor, elector, fellow-monks, Aristotle, Tetzel, Zwingli, the government, dress, scholasticism, humanism, art, music, the Catholic penance-system, poor preaching, mendicants, fast-days, masses, pilgrimages, the Bible (e.g. James, Jude, Job, Hebrews, Apocalypse, Mosaic authorship, etc.), public-worship, inadequate education, jurists, saint and relic worship, the prevailing methods of Biblical exegesis, excessive eating and drinking, the revered custom of kissing the pope's feet, Satan, Rome, Wittenberg, bad beer, marriage, dancing,—what was it that failed to elicit from him some complaint and criticism? There was hardly a subject to be thought, which escaped the terrific judgment of his tongue and pen.

Passages above cited might well be quoted in connection with this discussion. Yet, still others may be added:

> Willy nilly, I am compelled to become every day more learned, with so many and such able masters vying with one another to improve my mind. Some two years ago I wrote a little book on indulgences, which I now deeply regret having published; for at the time I was still sunk in a mighty superstitious veneration for the Roman tyranny.— Nor was this to be wondered at, for I was then engaged single-handed in my Sisyphean task.—Would to God I might prevail upon the book-sellers and upon all my

readers to burn up the whole of my writings on indulgences and to substitute for them this propostion: "Indulgences are a knavish Trick of the Roman Sycophants."—I now know of a certainty that the papacy is the kingdom of Babylon—.[1]

A certain Italian friar of Cremona has written a "Revocation of Martin Luther to the Holy See"—that is, a revocation in which not I revoke anything (as the words declare) but he revokes me. That is the kind of Latin the Italians are now beginning to write.[2]

I am attacking a difficult matter, and one perhaps impossible to abate, since it has become so firmly entrenched through century-long custom and the common consent of men that it would be necessary to abolish most of the books now in vogue, to alter well-nigh the whole external form of the churches, and to introduce, or rather reintroduce, a totally different kind of ceremonies. But my Christ lives; and we must be careful to give more heed to the Word of God than to all the thoughts of men and of angels. I will perform the duties of my office, and uncover the facts in the case; I will give the truth as I have received it, freely and without malice. For the rest let every man look to his own salvation.[3]

But you will say: How is this? Will you not overturn the practice and teaching of all the churches and monasteries, by virtue of which they have flourished these many centuries? For the mass is the foundation of their anniversaries, intercessions, applications, communications, etc.—that is to say, of their fat income. I answer: This is the very thing that has constrained me to write of the captivity of the Church, for in this manner the adorable testament of God has been subjected to the bondage of a godless traffic, through the opinions and traditions of wicked men, who, passing over the Word of God, have put forth the thoughts of their own hearts and misled the whole world. *What do I care for the number and influence of those who are in this error?* The truth is mightier than they all.—I am uttering unheard-of and startling things; but if you will consider the meaning of the mass, you will realize that I have spoken the truth.[4]

O unhappy, all who bear the name of priest today! They not only do not know nor do what becometh priests, but they are ignorant of what they ought to know and do. They fulfil the saying in Isaiah 56: "His watchmen are all blind, they are all ignorant; the shepherds themselves knew no understanding; all have declined into their own way, everyone after his own gain".[5]

By what right, in God's name, does the pope impose his laws upon us?[6]

—I lift my voice and confidently cry: No laws may by any right be laid upon Christians, whether by men or angels, without their consent: for we are free from all things.[7]

The pope decrees—that marriage is dissolved if one party enters a monastery even without the consent of the other, provided the marriage be not yet consummated. Gramercy, what devil puts such monstrous things into the pope's mind![8]

Not only is marriage regarded as a sacrament without the least warrant of Scripture, but the very traditions which extol it as a sacrament have turned it into a farce.[9]

I can scarce contain myself when I contemplate the wicked tyrannies of these desperate men, who with their farcical and childish fancies mock and overthrow the liberty and the glory of the Christian religion. Let every one, therefore, who knows himself to be a Christian be assured of this, and apply it to himself,—that we are all priests, and there is no difference between us;—[10]

I have indeed sharply inveighed against ungodly teachings in general, and *I have not been slow to bite my adversaries,* not because of their immorality, but because of their ungodliness. And of this *I repent so little* that I have determined to persevere in that fervent zeal, and to despise the judgment of men.—*What is the good of salt if it does not bite?*[11]

—Our friend Helt (prior at Wittenberg) is a fine ruler and organizer—of the kitchen, for he cares chiefly for the belly; perhaps he will care more for his head later.—[12]

Rome is a harlot. I would not take a thousand gulden not to have seen it, for I never would have believed the true state of affairs from what other people told me, had I not seen it myself. The Italians mocked us for being pious monks, for they hold Christians fools. They say six or seven masses in the time it takes me to say one, for they take money for it and I do not. The only crime in Italy is poverty. They still punish homicide and theft a little, for they have to, but no other sin is too gross for them—.[13]

(Luther)—I liked your sermon right well, friend Bucer, and yet I think mine was better.

(Bucer)—I gladly admit your superiority, doctor.

(Luther)—I don't mean to boast, I know my weakness and that I am not so acute and learned as you in my sermons. But when I enter the pulpit, I consider my audience—mostly poor laymen and Wends, and preach to them. Like a mother I try to give my children milk, and not some fine syrup from the apothecary. You preach over their heads, floating around in the clouds and in the "shpirit."[14]

Ecclesiastes has neither boots nor spurs, but rides in socks, as I did when I was in the cloister.[15]

Many sweat to reconcile St. Paul and St. James, as does Melanchthon in his Apology, but in vain. "Faith justifies" and "faith does not justify" contradict each other flatly. If any one can harmonize them I will give him my doctor's hood and let him call me a fool.

Let us banish this epistle from the university, for it is worthless. It has no syllable about Christ, not even naming him except once at the beginning. I think it was written by some Jew who had heard of the Christians but not joined them. James had learned that the Christians insisted strongly on faith in Christ and so he said to himself: "Well, you must take issue with them and speak only of works," and so he does. He says not a word of the passion and resurrection of Christ, the text of all the other apostles. Moreover, he has no order nor method. He speaks now of clothes, now of wrath, jumping from one topic to another. He has this simile: "For as the body without the spirit is dead, so faith without works is dead also." Mary, mother of God! He compares faith to the body when it should rather be compared to the soul! The ancients saw all this and did not consider the epistle canonical.[16]

St. John's Gospel and his first epistle, St. Paul's epistles, and especially Romans, Galatians, and Ephesians, and St. Peter's first epistle are the books which teach all that is necessary for salvation, even if you read no other books. In comparison with them, James is a right straw epistle, for it has no evangelic manner about it.[17]

In this regard my advice would be that Aristotle's "Physics", "Metaphysics", "On the Soul", "Ethics", which have hitherto been thought his best books, should be altogether discarded, together with all the rest of his books which boast of treating the things of nature, although nothing can be learned from them either of the things of nature or the things of the Spirit.—I venture to say that any potter has more knowledge of nature than is written in these books. It grieves me to the heart that this damned, conceited, rascally heathen has with his false words deluded and made fools of so many of the best Christians. God has sent him as a plague upon us for our sins.[18]

It would be natural to suppose that one who thus approaches everything under such critical analysis, would suffer from lack of an easy faith. Skepticism and a critical-temper go well hand in hand. This is just what appears, peculiarly enough, in Luther.

Cordatus in his "Tagebuch über—Luther"[19] quotes him as having said "Si tantum fidem haberem, quantam deberem, szo wolt ich den Teucken langst irschlagen haben, und die Tyrannen kurre haben gemacht. Ich habe mich wol szo mit yhnen zuplagt. Sed fides diest mihi—."[20] Again:[21] "At lieber Gott, art. fidei wil nicht ein. Ideo tot accidunt tristiciae. Saepe mihi irascor, quod toties praelegi, praedicavi, scripsi de vincenda hac tentatione, et temptatus non possum extinguere tristicias,—.[22]

From all this we see the man of intellectual and discriminating vigor; a philosophical mind, a logician and a dialectician, if necessary; an independent thinker and a nonconformist; a thorough-going critic. Likewise, as we found it hard to think of him as both a mystic and a practical man, two traits seldom found together in so marked a manner in one and the same personality.—so, too, here with all his keen sense of criticism and power to evaluate, to find that he was tremendously superstitious and given to fall into naive and undiscriminating acquiescence wherein his critical-temper failed to function. We might say that it is again the tendencies to objective-mindedness and to subjective-mindedness that have come to cross swords. The superstitious in Luther cannot be explained in so simple a fashion as to say that he was completely influenced by the superstitious ideas, traditions, and beliefs of his day and age, for then what are we to say as to his critical temper which launched him out and above the generally accepted molds of his day and marked him as a very unique individual? The problem on our hands is to account for the naive, the non-philosophic, non-critical, the almost childish in his nature which was expressed in him as characteristic of him as the critical-temper which we have discussed. The superstitious with him is not a mold which was laid upon him from the outside, but has its roots in an opposite trait in his mental make-up: in the strong tendency found in him to introspection, the sensitive, the highly suggestible, the mystical strains which were continually seeking expression and which contributed to make him a credulous and at times unreflective temper, opposing the contradictory strains expressed by his critical minded-ness and incredulity.

Throughout his life he revealed the tendency to attribute what he could not explain to supernatural causes. Even a thunderstorm transcends natural phenomena. He said of one: "It is simply satanic. I believe the devils wanted to have a dispute and that some angel interposed this *chasma* and so tore their propositions up." Says Dr. Preserved Smith: "Sometimes his credulity takes an active form which shocks our modern humanity. He advised, for example, that a poor girl who was said to shed tears of blood in the presence of another woman be tortured as a witch. His advice as to how to frustrate the machinations of the spirits who stole the milk is more disgusting, though less cruel. Sometimes he took a rational view as when he said the stars did not influence events."[23]

Professor McGiffert gives an illuminating historical setting of the young Martin in the early years of his life when the young mind is highly impressionable and open to suggestions: Luther's mother "was imaginative and sensitive, the prey of all sorts of conflicting emotions, and she lived in devout and fearsome bondage to much that her husband must have laughed at. Mansfeld, with its somber woods and cavernous hills, was a congenial haunt of gnomes and fairies. Of the blacker sort they were apt to be. 'In the mines,' as Luther once said, 'the devil teases and deceives people, makes a racket, and calls up specters before

their eyes until they think they see a great
heap of ore and pure silver where there is none
at all. For if he can bewitch and fool men even
above ground, by clear day, in the light of the
sun, so that things look other than they are, he
can do it still better in the mines.' Margarethe
felt *the spell of the evil spirits, and their terror
long lingered with the boy Martin.* On one occasion she thought herself and her children
bewitched by an unfriendly neighbor, and
there was much ado to escape the curse."[24]

So, the growing mind was tutored amidst
imaginative beings, demons, good and bad
angels and the like. The thunderstorm experience in his early youth is well-known. In that
experience he felt a divine call. "Help, dear
Saint Anne! I will become a monk." His ab-
normally sensitive and apprehensive experiences in the monastery with his strict and
model asceticism are also well-known. The
sight of the crucifix, he said, frightened him
like a thunderbolt! He wrestled hard with the
devil, at one time throwing an ink-stand at
the supposed Satanic presence. "Oh, my sin,
my sin, my sin" he cried in agony as he sought
peace within the convent walls.[25]

But the mature Luther of the Reformer type
is the Luther we are especially interested in
considering. The Critical and Active Leader
and Organizer! The bold and fearless Antagonist of the world's greater powers! Has the
superstitious in him fled with the pre-philos-

ophic level of his younger mind? His own pen
is our best reply:

Luther to Spalatin
                            Wittenberg, August 19, 1527
Grace and peace.—A pestilence has broken
out here, but it is rather mild. Still it is
wonderful to see how men are terrified and
put to flight. I have never before seen such
a prodigy of Satanic power, so greatly is he
terrifying everybody. Nay, he is glad that
he can so frighten men's hearts and thus
scatter and destroy this one university which
he hates above all others, not without reason.—I am staying here, and it is necessary
that I do so because of the terrible fear
among the common people. Bugenhagen
and I are here alone with the deacons, but
Christ is present too, that we may not be
alone, and He will triumph in us over that
old serpent, murderer and sin-maker, however much he may bruise His heel—.[26]

Luther to Wenzel Link at Nuremberg.
                            (Wittenberg) July 14, 1528
Grace and peace in Christ.—My opinion of
lunatics is, that all idiots and insane persons are possessed by devils, though on
that account they will not be damned; but I
think Satan tries men in different ways,
some severely, some lightly, some for a
long time, some for a short one. Physicians
may attribute such things to natural causes,
and sometimes partly cure them by medicine, but they are ignorant of the power of

devils. Christ did not hesitate to say in the Gospel that the old woman bowed down with infirmity was bound by Satan, and Peter asserts that all whom Christ cured were possessed by devils so I am forced to believe, that many are made dumb, deaf and lame by Satan's malice, nor can I doubt that pestilence, fever, and other severe illnesses are caused by devils, who also bring on tempests, conflagrations and blights in fruit and grain. What wonder if these wicked angels scourge the human race with all kinds of harm and peril as much as God permits? If some are cured by herbs and other natural remedies, it is by God's mercy. I suppose a physician would have said that the sufferings Satan caused Job were due to natural agents and could be cured by natural remedies. So I believe your lunatics are tempted by Satan for a time. Indeed, does not Satan make those lunatics whose hearts he fills with fornication, murder, rapine and all evil lusts? He has more power over us than some think; especially over the saints, since he buffeted Paul and carried Christ where he would.—[27]

Luther to John Ruhel at Mansfeld

Seeburg, May 4, 1525

Grace and peace in Christ.—This matter concerns me deeply, *for the devil wishes to kill me.* I see that he is angry that hitherto he has been able to accomplish nothing either by fraud or force; *he thinks that if he were only free of me he could do as he liked*

and confound the whole world together, so
I almost believe that I am the cause that the
devil can do such things in the world, whereby God punishes it.—How fairly the devil
decks himself and his murderers!—If I can
do it before I die, I will yet take my Katie
to wife to spite the devil—.[28]

"When Schlaginhaufen," writes Preserved
Smith, "fainted on December 31, 1531, Luther
indulged in a violent invective against the
malice of Satan, and prescribed various
methods of fooling him. When restored to a
semi-conscious state, the victim of the diabolic
machination could only groan out 'My sins!
my sins!' but a quarter of an hour more of exhortation and ghostly comfort finally enabled
him to rise and go home."[29]

Dietrich nursed Luther through the severe
illness which attacked him after the Diet of
Augsburg in 1530. "If we may believe the man
of God," writes the same author, "this affliction was due to the direct interposition of the
devil, whom he saw in the form of a fiery snake
hanging from the roof of a neighboring tower.
With his habitual shiftiness, however, the old
Serpent changed his form into that of a star
when Luther endeavored to point him out to
his disciple."[30]

Another striking instance of the superstitious in the personality of the Great Reformer
is from the letter written to John Ruhel at Mansfeld, dated, Wittenberg, May 23, 1525:

—My gracious Lord, the Elector, passed away on the day I left you, between five and six o'clock, almost at the very time that Osterhausen was destroyed. He died in a gentle spirit.—We buried him without masses and vigils, and yet with fitting ceremony. Some stones were found in his lungs, and especially some in the gall, which is strange. They were almost as large as a shilling and half as thick as one's little finger.—Thus *his death* was Christianlike and blessed. *The sign of it was a rainbow that Philip and I saw* over Lockau one night last winter, *and a child born here at Wittenberg without a head; also another with club feet.*—[31]

From the Table-Talk we glean some interesting remarks attributed to Luther:[32]

Experience has proved the toad to be endowed with valuable qualities. If you run a stick through three toads, and, after having dried them in the sun, apply them to any pestilent tumor, they draw out all the poison, and the malady will disappear.[33]

I believe that the devil is in parrots, monkeys and apes, because they are able to imitate men so well.[34]

Many demons are in the woods, the waters, in swamps and in deserts, in order to hurt men. Others, in the dense clouds, cause tempests, thunder and hail and infect the atmosphere. But philosophers and scientists ascribe these phenomena to nature and I know not what causes.[35]

On the superstitious in Luther, Professor Heinrich Böhmer writes thus: "This firm belief in devils and witches was transmitted to Doctor Martinus in the same undiminished degree as the inexhaustible stock of popular sayings and stories, abuse and ridicule, which his father and mother had at their disposal. In fact, it was materially increased during his days at school and his stay in the monastery. Hence as a mature man Luther never merely postulates the possible instance: 'If devils all the world should fill,' no, the world to him is actually full of devils. These bad spirits are busy in house and yard, wood and field, about man and in man.—Such witches often pursued also Doctor Luther and his Katie. Small wonder, therefore, that the Doctor occasionally threatens these impudent instruments of the Devil even from the pulpit.—The consciousness of having continually to fight with the master of this world, but of always being able to fell him with a single word only serves to increase the Doctor's joyful feeling of strength. More than any other person he confirms the statement of Goethe: 'Superstition is the heritage of energetic and noble natures.'—This popular belief in devils and angels which he had imbibed with his mother's milk the Reformer tenaciously retained during his whole life."[36]

It is a gross misinterpretation of the personality of the Reformer to think, as said before, of him merely as a pawn moved by the superior forces of the existing superstitious beliefs; to be sure the impressions made on him during his early environment and the persisting beliefs of his contemporaries had their tremendous influence. Yet, we maintain, that the true understanding of this expressive side of his nature, is to be found in a deep-lying current of his mental-make-up which found an affinity with the mysterious and subtleties of life. Otherwise, his critical-temper would soon have banished even these accepted beliefs. The critical and the superstitious, opposite as they are, have in him deep-going roots and tendrils in the peculiar make-up of his rich nature and personality.

NOTES AND REFERENCES

[1]Th. Ribot, *Diseases of Personality* (Open Court Publishing Co., 1895 English Translation), p. 112, 126ff.

Section 1.   Self-Exaltation—Self-Abnegation

[2]Quoted by A. C. McGiffert, *Martin Luther, The Man and His Work* (New York: Century Co., 1917), p. 4.

[3]*Idem,* p. 14.
[4]*Idem,* p.16.
[5]*Idem,* p. 15.
[6]*Idem,* p. 39.
[7]*Idem,* p. 48.
[8]Preserved Smith, *Life and Letters of Martin Luther,* p. 26.

[9]Preserved Smith, *Luther's Correspondence and Other Contemporary Letters* (Philadelphia: Lutheran Publication Society, 1913), Vol. I, p. 60.

[10]*Idem,* pp. 76-77.

[11]Quoted by McGiffert, *op. cit.,* p. 97.

[12]*Idem,* p. 119.

[13]Letter to John Lang at Erfurt, Oct., 1516. Smith, *Life and Letters of Martin Luther,* pp. 32-33.

[14]Dec. 1530, P. Smith, *op. cit.,* p. 331.

[15]Michelet, *Life of Martin Luther,* p. 148

[16]P. Smith, *op. cit.* p. 264.

[17]May, 1527, Letter to Link, P. Smith, *Luther's Correspondence,* etc., Vol. II, p. 398.

[18]Smith, *Life and Letters of Martin Luther, op. cit.,* p. 333.

[19]*Idem,* p. 334.

[20]*Werke,* Weim. ed., 23, p. 278. Erl, Ed., 30, p. 148.

[21]Letter to Spalatin, 1519. Smith, *Luther's Correspondence,* Vol. I, p. 169.

[22]July, 1518, Letter to Link. Smith, *Idem,* p. 98.

[23]Smith, *Life and Letters of Martin Luther,* p. 331.

[24]Smith, *Luther's Correspondence,* Vol. I, p. 98.

[25]*Idem.,* pp. 191-192, (May 30, 1519).

[26]McGiffert, *Martin Luther,* p. 187.

[27]Knights of the Round-Table, i. e., students and friends who sat around the Reformer in conversation, as e. g., Conrad Cordatus, John Schlaginhaufen, Veit Dietrich, Anton Lauterbach, Jerome Weller, John Mathesius, Antonius Coronus, Magister Plato, John Stolz, Caspar Heydenreich, Jerome Besold, John Aurifaber.

On the value of the written records of these reporters as bearing witness to the genuine Luther, see a brief discussion by Heinrich Böhmer, *Luther in the light of Recent Research* (Translated by Carl

F. Huth '16), pp. 189-192. For a more complete discussion of the critical value of these records of the Table-Talk see Preserved Smith, *Luther's Table-Talk—A Critical Study,* in Vol. XXVI, 1907, No. 2, (Columbia University Studies).

Passages from these table-talk records we set down in this study as of value for the insight given us as a total-impression which Luther made upon his contemporaries.

[28]*Luther's Table-Talk* by Aurifaber, tr. by Wm. Hazlett, Esq., No. 412.

[29]Aurifaber, *op. cit.,* No. 408.

[30]*Idem,* No. 421.

[31]*Idem,* No. 423.

[32]*Idem,* No. 470.

[33]*Idem,* No. 498.

[34]Lauterbach, *Tagebuch,* p. 131.

[35]Supplied by him? (1540) Mathesius, *Tischreden,* p. 108.

[36]Cordatus, *Tagebuch,* p. 363ff.

[37]Quoted in McGiffert, *op. cit.,* p. 139.

[38]*Idem,* pp. 97-98.

[39]*Idem,* pp. 116-117.

[40]Quoted by McGiffert, *op. cit.,* p. 122.

[41]*Works of Martin Luther* (Holman Co., 1915), Vol. II, pp. 61-62.

[42]*Idem,* Vol. II, pp. 63-65.

[43]*Idem,* Vol. II, pp. 163-164.

[44]McGiffert, *op. cit.,* p. 170.

[45]*Idem,* p. 192.

[46]*Idem,* p. 192.

[47]*Idem,* p. 192.

[48]Quoted by McGiffert, *op. cit.,* p. 215.

[49]*Works of Martin Luther, op. cit.,* Vol. II, pp. 399-400.

[50]Quoted by McGiffert, *op. cit.*, pp. 346-347.

[51]Quoted by Smith, *Life and Letters of Martin Luther, op. cit.*, p. 337.

[52]Quoted in *Life of Luther* by Julius Köstlin, pp. 542-543.

[53]P. Smith and Herbert Percival Gallinger, *Conversations With Luther,* pp. 180-181.

[54]*Luther's Correspondence,* etc., Smith-Jacobs, *op. cit.*, Vol. II, pp. 244-246.

[55]E. g., Letter to Justus Jonas, Nov. 11th, 1527, quoted by Smith, *Life and Letters of Martin Luther, op. cit.*, p. 189.

Section 2.   Cruelty—Kindliness

[1]Quoted by McGiffert, *op. cit.*, p. 51.

[2]*Idem,* p. 73.

[3]Smith, *Life and Letters of Martin Luther, op. cit.*, p. 26.

[4]McGiffert, *op. cit.*, p. 63.

[5]Quoted by McGiffert, *op. cit.*, p. 71.

[6]*Idem,* p. 152.

[7]*Idem.,* pp. 154-155.

[8]Quoted by McGiffert, *op. cit.*, p. 155.

[9]P. Smith, *Luther's Correspondence,* etc., *op. cit.*, Vol. I, pp. 286-288.

[10]*Idem*—Letter to Link, p. 399, Vol. II, Smith-Jacobs.

[11]Smith, *Luther's Correspondence, op. cit.*, Vol. I, pp. 414-415.

[12]*Idem,* Smith-Jacobs, Vol. II, pp. 444-445.

[13]Quoted by Smith, *Life and Letters of Martin Luther, op. cit.*, p. 326.

[14]Opening sentences to one of Luther's Hymns— quoted by Morris Jastrow, *The Study of Religion* (London: Walter Scott, 1901), p. 14.

[15]Smith, *Life and Letters of Martin Luther, op. cit.,* p. 400.

[16]Quoted by McGiffert, *op. cit.,* pp. 162-163 (1520).

[17]Quoted by Smith, *Life and Letters of Martin Luther, op. cit.,* pp. 361-362.

[18]Quoted by McGiffert, *op. cit.,* p. 345.

[19]On the value of these table-talks, see reference 27 on pages 153-154.

[20]*Luther's Table Talk,* John Aurifaber, No. 495.

[21]*Idem,* No. 482.

[22]*Idem,* No. 427.

[23]*Idem,* No. 459.

[24]*Idem,* No. 111.

[25]*Idem,* No. 400.

[26]Mathesius, *Tischreden,* p. 88

[27]Schlagenhaufen, *Aufzeichnungen,* pp. 135-136.

[28]Quoted by McGiffert, *op. cit.,* pp. 151-152 (1531).

[29]*Idem,* pp. 51-52.

[30]Smith, *Luther's Correspondence, etc., op. cit.,* Vol. I, pp. 74-75.

[31]*Idem,* Vol. I, Appendix, p. 570.

[32]Cf. McGiffert, *op. cit.,* p. 199.

[33]*Idem,* p. 3.

[34]*Idem,* pp. 104-105.

[35]This lengthy quotation is found in Smith, *Life and Letters of Martin Luther, op. cit.,* pp. 353-354.

[36]Smith-Jacobs, *Luther's Correspondence, op. cit.,* Vol. II, p. 451.

[37]Letter to his wife, Katie. Quoted by McGiffert, *op. cit.,* p. 302.

[38]Gustav Freytag, *Martin Luther,* translated by Heinemann (Open Court Publishing Company), p. 104.

[39]Quoted by McGiffert, *op. cit.,* pp. 302-303.

⁴⁰*Cf*. Smith, *Life and Letters of Martin Luther, op. cit.,* p. 355.

⁴¹*Cf.* Smith, *Luther's Table-Talk—A Critical Study,* (New York: Columbia University Studies, 1907), Vol. XXVI, No. 2, p. 29.

⁴²*Idem,* p. 30.

⁴³McGiffert, *op. cit.,* p. 292.

Section 3. Humor—Melancholy

¹*Cf.* Smith, *Luther's Table-Talk—A Critical Study, op. cit.,* p. 95.

²Quoted by McGiffert, *op. cit.,* p. 29.

³"Humorn är en säkerhetsventil, dubbelt nödvändig i ett liv, utsatt för ett högtryck, som utan humorns avledning skulle spränga även en hjältesjäl." *Humor och Melankoli och Andra Lutherstudier,* Nathan Söderblom (Stockholm, 1919) p. 6. This notable volume written by the Archbishop of the State Church (Lutheran) of Sweden is an important scholarly contribution and interpretation to the study of Luther's personality. It has not yet been translated (1923).

⁴December 7, 1519, Smith, *Luther's Correspondence, op. cit.,* Vol. I, pp. 257-261.

⁵*Cf.* Nathan Söderblom, *op. cit.,* p. 8, and Smith, *Life and Letters of Martin Luther, op. cit.,* p. 365. Luther was made fun of by his foes for this incident and all sorts of stories circulated. In a letter to George Spalatin, October 13, 1519, he says: "Had they dared they would have said that I wore the flowers on my head. I neither can nor wish to prevent all such stories." Smith, *Luther's Correspondence, etc., op. cit.,* Vol. I, p. 224.

⁶Quoted in Smith, *Life and Letters of Martin Luther, op. cit.,* p. 118.

[7]*Cf.* Dr. Nathan Söderblom, *op. cit.,* p. 9.

[8]Aleander to the Vice-Chancellor Cardinal d' Medici at Rome, Smith, *Luther's Correspondence, etc., op. cit.,* Vol. I, p. 527.

[9]Quoted by McGiffert, *op. cit.,* p. 200.

[10]*Idem,* p. 197.

[11]Smith, *Life and Letters of Martin Luther, op. cit.,* p. 248.

[12]Quoted by Smith, *Life and Letters of Martin Luther, op. cit.,* pp. 249-250. Note how similar, both as revealing his quaint humor and his love of nature, is the following letter:

To Wolfgang Sieberger at Wittenberg

(Wittenberg, Autumn, 1534)

Complaint of the Birds to Luther against Wolfgang.

We, thrushes, blackbirds, finches, linnets, goldfinches, and all other pious, honorable birds, who migrate this autumn over Wittenberg, give your kindness to know, that we are credibly informed that one Wolfgang Sieberger, your servant, has conceived a great wicked plot against us, and has bought some old, rotten nets very dear, to make a fowling-net out of anger and hatred to us. He undertakes to rob us of the freedom God has given us to fly through the air, and he puts our lives in danger, a thing we have not deserved of him. All this, as you yourself can imagine, is a great trouble and danger to us poor birds, who have neither houses nor barns nor anything else, and so we humbly and kindly pray you to restrain your servant, or, if that cannot be, at least to cause him to strew corn on the fowling-net in the evening and not to get up in the morning before eight, so that we can continue our journey over Wittenberg. If he will not do this, but keeps on wickedly seeking our lives, we will pray God to plague him, and instead of us to send frogs, locusts, and snails into the fowling-net by day and at night to give him mice, fleas, lice, and bugs, so that he will forget us and leave us free. Why does he not use his wrath and industry against sparrows, swallows, magpies, crows, ravens, mice, and rats? They do you much harm, rob and steal corn, oats, and barley even out of the houses, whereas we only eat crumbs and a stray grain or two of wheat. We leave our case to right reason whether he has not done us wrong. We hope to God, that as many of our brothers and friends escaped from him, we too, who saw his dirty old nets yesterday, may also escape from them.

Written in our lofty home in the trees with our usual quill and seal.

Behold the fowls of the air: for they sow not, neither do they reap nor gather into barns; yet your heavenly Father feedeth them. Are ye not much better than they? Matthew vi, 26. (Quoted by Smith, *op. cit.,* pp. 360-361.)

Wolfgang Sieberger was a student whom Luther had befriended, and who, unsuccessful in studies, had gone into the profession of fowler which in turn proved to be an unsuccessful enterprise. Luther did not hesitate to tease and poke fun at his young friend!

[13]Smith, *Life and Letters of Martin Luther, op. cit.,* pp. 324-325. Letter to Jerome Weller at Wittenberg, 1530.

[14]This lengthy quotation is from Smith, *Life and Letters of Martin Luther, op. cit,* pp. 325-326.

[15]*Idem,* p. 353.

[16]Quoted by McGiffert, *op. cit.,* p. 55.

[17]Smith, *Life and Letters of Martin Luther, op. cit.,* p. 319.

[18]*Idem,* p. 357.

[19]It would be interesting, indeed, to lengthen the list of evidences of this trait in Luther, which here we have included under the name of "humor," such as those profuse illustrations in the *Table-Talk,* but space forbids in a discussion where other cross-currents need consideration.

[20]"As soon as a violent fit of anger rouses Luther's blood the humorous poet in him begins to stir." Prof. Heinrich Böhmer: *Luther in Light of Recent Research* (New York: Christian Herald, 1916), p. 196.

[21]For further illustrations see Böhmer, *op. cit.,* p. 196.

[22]*Cf.* the play on the Trinity, p. 96 of this book.

[23]Quoted above on p. 86.

[24]Smith-Jacobs, *Luther's Correspondence, op. cit.,* Vol. II, p. 428.

[25]Letter to Melanchthon, August 2, 1527, Smith-Jacobs, *Luther's Correspondence, op. cit.,* Vol. II, p. 409.

[26]Letter to John Agricola at Eisleben, August 21, 1527, *Idem,* Vol. II, p. 412.

[27]Letter to Melanchthon, *Idem,* Vol. II, p. 419.

[28]Letter to Nicholas Hausmann, November 7, 1527, *Idem,* Vol. II, p. 420.

[29]Letter to Justus Jonas, November 11 (?), 1527, *Idem,* Vol. II, pp. 420-422.

[30]Letter to Wenzel Link, November 22, 1527, *Idem,* Vol. II, pp. 423-424.

[31]Smith, *Life and Letters of Martin Luther, op. cit.,* pp. 338-339.

[32]Letter to George Mascov, Provost in Leitzkau-Wittenberg, last months of 1516. Smith, *Luther's Correspondence, op. cit.,* Vol. I, p. 50.

[33]Letter to John Staupitz, October 3, 1519, *Idem,* Vol. I, p. 220.

[34]Letter to Nicholas Hausmann at Zwickau, March 3, 1529, *Idem,* Smith-Jacobs, Vol. II, pp. 468-469.

[35]*Luther on Galatians,* (Philadelphia, John Highlands, 1891), pp. 178-181.

Prof. William James in his *The Varieties of Religious Experience,* pp. 244-246, quotes Luther in this Commentary on Galatians in an abridged form, as an example of the type of the extreme melancholic: "In the extreme of melancholy the self that consciously *is* can do absolutely nothing. It is completely bankrupt and without resource, and no works it can accomplish will avail." "Nothing in Catholic theology, I imagine, has ever spoken to sick souls as straight as this message from Luther's personal experience."

[36]June 19, 1530, Smith, *Life and Letters of Martin Luther, op. cit.,* p. 251.

[37]Quoted by McGiffert, *op. cit.,* p. 216.

[38]J. M. Reu, *Thirty-Five Years of Luther Research* (Chicago: Wartburg Publishing House, 1917), p. 97.

Section 4.   Practical-Temper—Mysticism

[1]McGiffert, *op. cit.,* p. 149.

[2]*Cf.* Smith, *Life and Letters of Martin Luther, op. cit.,* pp. 332-333.

[3]McGiffert, *op. cit.,* p. 301.

[4]In this letter Luther summarizes his view on the question much debated in the 16th Century, whether the taking of interest was permissible. It had been forbidden by the Canon law, but the prohibition was rapidly becoming a dead letter. Letter to Duke John Frederick of Saxony, June 18, 1524. Smith-Jacobs, *Luther's Correspondence, etc., op. cit.,* Vol. II, p. 237.

[5]Letter to Jerome Baumgartner at Nuremberg, October 12, 1524. *Idem,* Vol. II, pp. 257-258. (Luther took a keen interest in getting couples married!)

[6]Letter to Nicholas Hausmann in Zwickau, November 17, 1524, Smith-Jacobs, *Luther's Correspondence, op. cit.,* Vol. II, p. 259.

[7]Letter to the Elector Frederic, December 24, 1524, *Idem,* Vol. II, pp. 279-280.

[8]Letter to Nicholas Hausmann in Zwickau, March 26, 1525, *Idem,* Vol. II, pp. 298-299.

[9]May 1525, Smith-Jacobs, *Luther's Correspondence, op. cit.,* Vol. II, pp. 310-311.

[10]Luther's concern over the decline in the numbers of students at Wittenberg and the weakening of the faculty. Letter to Duke John Frederick of Electoral Saxony. Smith-Jacobs, *op. cit.,* Vol. II, p. 317 (1525).

[11]Letter to the Elector John of Saxony, October 31, 1525, Smith-Jacobs, *op. cit.,* Vol. II, pp. 342-343.

[12]*Idem,* Vol. II, pp. 353-354.

[13]Does not Luther show evidence here of psychological insight? Smith-Jacobs, *op. cit.,* Vol. II, p. 402.

[14]*Idem,* Vol. II, pp. 486-487.

[15]*Luther's Table Talk,* Aurifaber, No. 419. See footnote No. 27, pp. 153-154.

[16]*Idem,* No. 389.

[17]*Idem,* No. 397. Is not this and extract (foot-note 15) evidence for Luther's practical-homiletical ability?

[18]Quoted in Smith, *Life and Letters of Martin Luther, op. cit.,* p. 266.

[19]*Idem,* p. 187.

[20]*Idem,* p. 349.

[21]*Idem,* p. 350. Note the versatility and the practicality of his interests throughout!

²²*Works of Martin Luther,* (Holman, Philadelphia, 1915), Vol. II, pp. 61-164 abridged.

²³*Cf.* the interesting sketches found in McGiffert's *Martin Luther, The Man and His Work,* e.g. pp. 29, 53, 61, 63, 67, 68, 74, 89. "He had the true reformer's conscience—the sense of responsibility *for others as well as for himself,* and the true reformer's vision of the better things that ought to be.—In any crowd of bystanders he would have been first to go to the rescue where need was, and quickest to see the need not obvious to all. The aloofness of the mere observer was not his; he was too completely one with all he saw to stand apart and let it go its way alone." (p. 66)

²⁴Quoted by Henry Eyster Jacobs in "Martin Luther" of the series *Heroes of the Reformation,* edited by Samuel Macauley Jackson, pp. 196-197, with the support of Erlangen, 64:289 *sqq.*

²⁵Quoted from James F. Lambert, *Luther's Hymns* (Philadelphia: General Council Publication House, 1917), pp. 40-41.

²⁶King James Version.

²⁷*Luther on Galatians* (Philadelphia: John Highlands, 1891), p. 170.

²⁸Smith, *Luther's Correspondence, op. cit.,* Vol. I, p. 48.

²⁹William James, *The Varieties of Religious Experience* (New York: Longmans, Green and Co., 1902), p. 382.

³⁰Quoted in G. H. Gerberding, *The Lutheran Pastor* (Philadelphia: Lutheran Publication Society, 1902), p. 201.

³¹Quoted in Seeburg, *op. cit.,* Vol. II, pp. 238-239.

³²*Idem,* p. 228.

³³*Idem,* pp. 232-233.

[34]*Luther's Table Talk,* Aurifaber, No. 182. See foot-note 27, pp. 153-154.

[35]*Idem,* No. 186.

[36]*Idem,* No. 236.

[37]Quoted by Professor Dewey in his *German Philosophy and Politics* (New York: Henry Holt Co., 1915), pp. 17-18. For a more detailed study of Luther's mysticism, see the little volume entitled *Psychological Studies in Lutheranism* by Paul Harold Heisey. (Burlington, Iowa: The German Literary Board, 1916), especially Chapter II, "A Study in the Mysticism of Luther," pp. 39-95.

Section 5.   Critical-Temper—Superstition

[1]*Works of Martin Luther, ed. cit.,* Vol. II, "The Babylonian Captivity of the Church," pp. 170-171.

[2]*Idem,* p. 171. Here Luther's keen and critical mind takes up and pokes fun at the use of "revocatio" with an objective genitive.

[3]*Idem,* pp. 194-195.

[4]*Idem,* pp. 209-210.

[5]*Idem,* pp. 219-220.

[6]*Idem,* p. 233.

[7]*Idem,* p. 235.

[8]*Idem,* p. 243.

[9]*Idem,* p. 257.

[10]*Idem,* pp. 282-283. (To appreciate the revolutionary character of this statement, one must remember the great hierarchical system of Luther's day!)

[11]"A Treatise on Christian Liberty" with "Letter to Pope Leo X" (1520), *Idem,* Vol. II, p. 302.

[12]Smith, *Luther's Correspondence, op. cit.,* Vol. I, p. 192.

[13]Smith, *Life and Letters of Martin Luther, op. cit.,* p. 19. (Is not this a criticism that tends to excess?)

[14]*Idem,* p. 294, "Luther ridicules his guest's pronounciation of "Geist" (spirit) as "Gaischt.""

[15]*Idem,* p. 268.

[16]*Idem,* p. 269. Luther, the Bible Critic!

[17]*Idem,* p. 268.

[18]Again, does not his critical-temper lead him to excessive statements? (We note also the "cruel" in his nature here being expressed.) "An Open Letter to the Christian Nobility" *Luther's Works* (edition cited), Vol. II, p. 146.

[19]Cordatus, *Tagebuch über Dr. Martin Luther* (Halle: Max Niemeyer, 1885), p. 209, No. 823.

[20]"Had I such great faith as I ought to have, I should long ago have slain the Turk and curbed every tyrant. I have indeed tormented myself greatly about them. But my faith is wanting."

[21]No. 1652, p. 452 (On Cordatus and the "Table-Talk" see footnote No. 27, pp. 153-154.

[22]"O my God, the article on faith won't go home; hence so many sad moods arise. Often I have to take myself to task for failing to master such moods when they come, I who have so often taught in lectures, sermons and writings how such temptations are to be overcome."

[23]Smith, *Luther's Table Talk, op. cit.,* Columbia Univ. Studies, Vol. 26, pp. 108-109, No. 2.

[24]McGiffert, *op. cit.,* p. 7.

[25]As an example of the superstitious attitudes prevailing in Luther's day, a guide-book from his time has this to say about the origin of a certain church which Luther visited: "Where the church is, there once stood a great walnut tree in which devils made their home. Whoever happened to pass by they vilified and slandered, and no one knew who did it. It was revealed to St. Pascal the pope that he

should cut down the tree and build a church in its place to the honor of our dear Lady. The pope therefore went to the Porta Flamina with a great procession of clergy and laity and rooted the tree out of the earth. Under it there was found a coffin containing the body of the wicked Nero, who put St. Peter and St. Paul to death with many other Christians. The same Nero set fire to Rome in twelve places that he might see how great a conflagration it would make. The Romans consequently wished to put him in prison, but he stabbed himself, and was buried in the abovementioned place. Afterward Pope Pascal burned to ashes the body of the wicked Nero and the walnut tree, and exorcised all the devils that were in the tree, and built a church, which was called Maria del Popolo because of the multitude of people there." McGiffert, *op. cit.,* pp. 41-42.

[26]Smith-Jacobs, *Luther's Correspondence, op. cit.,* Vol. II, pp. 410-411.

[27]*Idem,* Vol. II, pp. 447-448.

[28]*Idem,* Vol. II, pp. 309-310.

[29]Smith, *Luther's Table Talk, op. cit.,* Vol. 26, No. 2, p. 24.

[30]*Idem,* p. 22.

[31]Smith-Jacobs, *Luther's Correspondence, op. cit.,* Vol. II, p. 318.

[32]See footnote 27, pp. 153-154.

[33]Aurifaber, *Luther's Table Talk, op. cit.,* No. 736.

[34]Smith and Herbert Percival Gallinger, *Conversations with Luther,* (Boston: Pilgrim Press, 1915), p. 163.

[35]*Idem,* p. 158.

[36]*Luther in Light of Recent Research,* Heinrich Böhmer (translated by Carl F. Huth, Jr.), Chapter VIII, "The Background of Luther's Life and Religion," pp. 256, 258, 259.

Chapter III

THE CO-ORDINATING AND INTEGRATING FACTOR IN THE PERSONALITY OF MARTIN LUTHER— A STUDY IN THE PSYCHOLOGY OF RELIGIOUS GENIUS

Further cross-currents in the Reformer's personality which are evident, would make interesting study, e.g., "independence—dependence"; "callousness—impressibility"; "imperiousness— regard"; "composure—restlessness"; "healthy-mindedness—sick-soul"; "freedom—restraint"; "optimism—pessimism"; and the list might still be lengthened!

It is characteristic with him that any of these currents are not mere superficialities which are blown upon him by winds of passing circumstance, but that they are rooted with tenacious fibers into the very depth of his personality. Each current had its tendency to excess. Each was very much alive. Each was marked with a high degree of intensity. Each claimed as its source: the inner and hidden recesses. Not fictitious and illusory but real forces. Not easily eradicated! Not easily suppressed! They formed real cross-currents. His whole soul was a constant battlefield, now with this and now with that strain; inconsistencies, re-enforce-

ments, agreements, disagreements, obstructions, surged up incessantly from the depths
of his soul. These conflicting tendencies increased to a more accentuated differentiation
as his mind developed; forced before the throne
of consciousness by their intensity, sooner or
later they must be co-ordinated; some bond of
vital association between them must somehow
be found, in order to save such a personality
from the threatening danger of a pathogenetic
disintegration. The extracts from his pen which
we have set down as illustrative of conflicting
tendencies, together with the intense life which
his biography discloses, present a serious type
of concrete personality.

This native mental constitution of Luther
may find itself explained in some measure in
terms of heredity and racial character which
lie in the background of all psycho-physical
organisms. A father full of vigor, courage, de-
termination, self-respect, self-restraint; sturdy,
honest, sane, independent, ambitious, indus-
trious, shrewd, religious, disciplined and dis-
ciplinary! A mother who was sensitive, imaginative, religious, emotional, quiet, strict,
cheerful, optimistic, and given to wholesome
humor! Their child must not be studied apart
from them! Whatever and however the inheritance, complex enough to be suggestive, the
peculiar mental endowment of the son was
initiated into the world with conflicting strains
which became a serious problem with him early

in life and which needed co-ordination. The chief battleground for him was not in the world outside, but the field of his own inner consciousness. His whole biography is the severe attempt at co-ordination and synthesis. Certainly his monastic life is inexplicable in other terms. The career that father and friends laid out for him took no cognizance of these inner and secret struggles. They must be met by him in his own necessary way. They must be met! That he bordered on disintegration and a pathogenetic condition not only once but at several distinct times, he has himself confessed. Mere tradition, custom, formal acquiescence, were not suited to his temper without a keen sense of personal appropriation. The struggling and insistent currents within him demanded such a co-ordination as could pass their bar and include them all.

The serious turn toward Religion is the path that such type of minds seek for their solutions. And it is the very nature of Religion to be such a court for difficulties, because of its wide range and comprehensiveness. Philosophy, the sciences, the trades, are too one-sided and narrow for such a temper. Neither will Religion in a too confined mold satisfy it. Martin was blessed with a mind that could have made a mark in many an inviting field. Philosophy, music, law, poetry, history, education, alone would have been benefited by his applying himself with his gifts to any of these inviting fields

awaiting the contributions of master-minds.
But in the midst of great progress, for example,
in the field chosen for him by his ambitious
father, the field of law, he suddenly astonishes
everyone by selling at a small price his expen-
sive books on law and turns his face towards
the dark walls of a monastery which promised
those who entered a life of withdrawal and
isolation. The struggles of his soul were real
and compelling. The Religion of his day
offered itself to him in a distinct mold. He tried
with all his might to find peace there. His one
aim was a synthesis for which his personality
cried. "If ever a monk gained heaven by his
monkery, I must have done so. All the brethren
who knew me will bear witness. For I should
have martyred myself, if I had kept it up longer,
with watching, praying, reading, and other
labors."[1]

But the many conflicting strains of his personality could not fit into the mold prevailing
in the Catholic religious system which was
presented to him "within the walls," and, none
else to try, and with a tremendous insistence
to find himself at peace,—he burst this shell
and clung to what he found to be the kernel
which promised satisfaction.

Luther has often been misinterpreted, even
by Protestant admirers, as having "found himself" in certain definite occasions, as e.g., "the
thunderstorm experience," the "Sancta Scala
episode," the "finding of a copy of the Sacred

Scriptures," the "reading of the passage in Romans I, 17: 'The just shall live by faith' ";— but this is a misreading! The synthesis which became effective with him was one of a growing and refining process which, indeed, became strengthened and cogently expressed on certain occasions but which required time and a history to become co-ordinated and integrated. His was not a cataclysmic synthesis but an ever developing and growing experience which was throwing light upon his pathway to further experience and final synthesis. Dr. Preserved Smith reaches a similar conclusion in the interpretation of this attempt at integration on Luther's part, when he remarks: "Of course Luther's development was not completed at once. Even after the master-key (Romans I, 17) had been found, the long struggle continued, and other factors entered in to modify and enrich his character. He entered the monastery to save his soul, (we might here say: to save his personality!), and the struggle for peace took twelve long years before the monk was ripe for the great deeds he was called on to perform. No one can get even an idea of what the struggle cost him save by reading after him the folios and quartos he perused, and trying to follow him in all that tangled labyrinth."[2]

What, then, was the Co-ordinating and Integrating Factor in his Personality? It is not always easy and even fair to give answer to such a question for someone else,—perhaps a simple answer is not only insufficient but partial. But, if pressed to state an answer, in simplest terms and to the least common denominator, to find the chief Co-ordinating and Integrating Factor, we will not go amiss in saying that what saved Luther from a complete disintegration and what brought him to the level of a wholesome and united personality and what lay hold of, elevated, refined and synthesized the currents in him to the making of the vigorous and enthusiastic leader and religious genius,—was a deep and unique and growing Christ-experience[3] which came to be for him the norm of human life in all its conflicting phases, the Holy of holies, and the power to conquer and subdue to proper proportions the opposing strains of his own mental battleground. With this growing experience came new light on the reasons why the religious molds of the day failed to satisfy him; and he, both by temperament and by nature, was destined to bring this illumination to others. It involved a stormy career for him, but the Integration was strong enough in the first and foremost place to unite all his powerful cross-currents, and deep enough to equip him for the awful fray into which he was to offer the strength of his entire personality!

Let it at once be noted, that the conflicting tendencies were not wiped off the slate with the coming of these great experiences of an appropriated Christ. They were related and made

subordinate and colored by the acquired en-
trenchment of this great and unique "warm
spot."[4] We have seen that the cross-currents
persist: the self-exaltative and the self-abnegative strains, the cruel and the kind, the
humorous and the melancholic, the practical
and the mystical, the critical and the superstitious (etc.). All these strains persist, indeed,
and continue to contribute to his personality.
But opposing as they are, they become, now,
processes that have been synthesized and uni-
fied under a common and acceptable bond
which acts as a regulative power and ensures
poise and balance.

We have remarked already, that in any normal individual there are ceaseless alterations
and re-combinations of the elements of the
self and that, as William James has pointed out,
the most characteristic fact of the self is just
these constant mutations that are going on
within it. We must also note that "the conscious
self at any moment is only a small part of the
entire personality, the larger share of which
is the sub-conscious self." Dr. Starbuck's analysis is very helpful in this connection: The
conscious self at any time is made up of the
drifting to the surface out of this great "sub-
merge" of the subconscious, of certain fairly
well organized cores or nuclei of related states
and processes. "The ego is not a fixed entity
that stands apart and watches the life processes go on." The Self is latent in every psycho-

sis and emerges when any group of processes is sufficiently organized and so far intensified as to form a warm spot in the somewhat diffuse group of experiences that cohere in the single organism. In the normal personality there are certain deep-going lines of organization that are fairly constant and give stability to the self. Figure I opposite illustrates the point. (It is drawn, following the suggestions of Prof. Starbuck.) The "enclosed space" represents the mass of subliminal processes while "A" and "B" represent integrated nuclei of conscious selves. In *Normal* Consciousness these two selves "A" and "B" will be so nearly coincident, due to the continuity and consistency in the stream of experiences, as to have almost everything in common "M". In *Double* Mindedness we have the condition of "A^1" and "B^1" with "M^1". The condition underlying Double-mindedness is: that two or more centres or related processes or selves may drift above the threshold of clear consciousness in rapid succession, while each is imperfectly cognizant of the other. Double-mindedness describes much in Morality and Religion that otherwise goes under the terms of "insincerity" and "hypocrisy". Under the heading of "The Value to Morality of Double-Mindedness" Dr. Starbuck remarks: "It is an instructive fact that the biography of so many moral and religious geniuses betrays a struggle between the cross-currents of the Self in the direction of good and

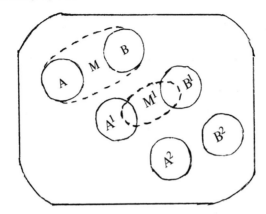

Figure I

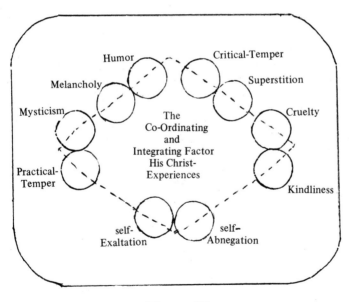

Figure II

evil." *Alternating* Personality: "A²" and "B²" have no common synthesis—no "M". It is a pathological condition.[5]

This analysis by Professor Starbuck on the phenomenon of "Double-Mindedness" in the human personality is extremely helpful in the understanding of the personality of Martin Luther, with his multiple and conflicting strains. His is the type of the "double-minded"! His is the type that has very marked "centres" which tend to express contradictions and may become pathological. We might represent Luther in the accompanying diagram (Figure II, page 175) which, on the basis of the foregoing discussion is self-illustrative. Diagrams are certainly inadequate in depicting such a complex phenomenon as the human personality, yet helpful as a total impression and revealing relationships. We have included only those strains discussed at length; many more circles of cross-currents may be added (as stated in the opening sentences of this chapter). The nuclei are not eradicated, but still remain, now tied together in a Large Synthesis under which each is subordinate and to which each contributes.

We now come to the problem to which this study has been directed: the problem of the Religious Genius. It is one which has troubled the minds of the admirers of the greater personalities. Studies have been made touching the possible relationship between heredity and the unique mental constitution, the possible relationship between insanity and genius, and again in trying to investigate what prominent characteristics go to make up unusual mental powers. Such a complex problem, indeed, needs to be bombarded from all possible and conceivable angles. The attack we have been attempting to make on the problem has been by attempting to tunnel into the mysteries of the subconscious by the light of the torch given in the conscious; by attempting to trace down the roots of the given contradictory traits and following the hint given by their expression to a rich sub-structure; by attempting to apprehend the relationship of variety to unity, of conflict to order, of opposition to harmony, of cross-currents to co-ordination and integration.

Many pairs of contradictory tendencies we have found in the mental constitution of the Great Reformer. Due to these contradictions there arises a tremendous conflict which forces the individual to achieve some kind of unification and synthesis. To be endowed with such a remarkable number and so powerful cross-currents, convinces us that it is of paramount necessity that, that individual must go through some real and live experiences, by trial and error, to perfect adjustment. To have reached a synthesis is to save his soul! But in saving himself, he has been gathering unto himself many and rich fruits through the experience. *The multiple elements of his turbulent mental constitution have enriched him.* He becomes a man not of one talent but of many. His type tends *from* the narrow and confined *to* the broad and universal. The rich and the varied background of his "self" gave him a many-sided view with a real appreciation of the various complex problems that go to make up life. Each current contributed to the enrichment of his personality and through this touched his career. The cruel in him made him a feared polemicist. The warm-hearted was needed to bring poise and balance and to keep him in sympathetic touch with his fellows; the self-exaltative gave him the much-needed sense of composure and confidence necessary to any innovator, the self-abnegative acted as a check to bring him to the sense of the tremendous responsibilities of his leadership and to conserve him from the extremes of radicalism. The critical in him made him capable of keen analysis and gave him the power to evaluate the problems before him which presented themselves oftentimes without precedent; the superstitious in him checked any tendency to cold rationalism; the practical gave him a good sense of observation to the things at hand and their need for reform, while the mystic in him brought out the aesthetic, the appreciative characteristic in him for the higher values that go to make up a wholesome life. The humorous in him was the gospel of relaxation from the stress and strain of unabated conflict, while

the melancholic turned him to a searching
self-examination and self-renewal. These
are but suggestive; the reader should fill out
the implications.

The cross-currents flowed as tributaries bearing with them their offering to the finally united
self. The world stands aghast as it contemplates
the many-sided interests of the man. A poet,
a philosopher, a musician, a dialectician, a
platform debater, an organizer, a sympathetic
pastor, an author, an exegete, a conversation-
alist,—one whose influence is measured in
centuries and who becomes the pivotal point
in human history. His type is not the stagnant
but the creative type. The activity of his life
finds its roots in the activity of his own inner
consciousness as it continually wrestled with
itself. The rich cross-currents plus the co-ordinating and integrating factor under which they
became organized is the psychological background which was making and creating in him
one of the world's greatest religious geniuses.
Genius, we are taught through the concrete
case of Martin Luther, therefore, is not the result of the supremacy and uniqueness of one
specialized trait, but it is rather the poise and
continued integrating of the many, the deep
although opposite and rich tendencies of the
human personality.

NOTES AND REFERENCES

¹Quoted by McGiffert, *op. cit.,* p. 27.

²Smith, *Life and Letters of Martin Luther, op. cit.,* p. 15.

³What this Christ-experience was *theologically, Christologically* or *metaphysically* is *not* the burden of this study. Our approach is limited to the *psychological* only.

⁴Borrowing Dr. Starbuck's term.

⁵Article by Prof. E. D. Starbuck, entitled "Double-Mindedness" in Hastings, *Encyclopedia of Religion and Ethics.*

BIBLIOGRAPHY

Adler, Alf., *The Neurotic Constitution.* (Outlines of a Comparative Individualistic Psychology and Psychotherapy), (Moffat, Yard, & Co., 1921).

Aurifaber, John, *Luther's Table-Talk,* translated by William Hazlitt, Esq. (Philadelphia, The Lutheran Publication Society).

Baldwin, J. M., *Dictionary of Philosophy and Psychology,* Article on "Personality, Disorders of."

Beers, Clifford W., *A Mind That Found Itself* (an autobiography), (New York, Longmans, Green & Co., 1908).

Binet, Alf., *Alterations of Personality* (New York, D. Appleton & Co., 1896).

Bohmer, Heinrich, *Luther in Light of Recent Research,* translated by Carl F. Huth, Jr. (New York, The Christian Herald, 1916).

Brentano, Franz, *Psychologie des Genies.*

Christie, Francis A., "Luther and Others," article in the *Harvard Theological Review,* April, 1912.

Cordatus, Conrad, *Tagebuch Über Dr. Martin Luther,* 1537 (Halle, Max Niemeyer, 1885).

Dau, W. H. T., *Luther Examined and Re-examined* (Concordia).

Dewey, John, *German Philosophy and Politics* (New York, Henry Holt Co., 1915).

Freud, Sigmund, *Psychopathology of Everyday Life,* (New York, The Macmillan Co.).

Freytag, Gustav, *Martin Luther,* translated by Heinemann (The Open Court Publishing Co.).

Galton, Fr., *Hereditary Genius and English Men of Science; Hereditary Genius* (New York, The Macmillan Co., 1892).

Gerberding, G. H., *The Lutheran Pastor* (Philadelphia, Lutheran Publication Society, 1902).

Goddard, H. H., *Psychology of the Normal and Subnormal* (New York, Dodd, Mead & Co., 1919).

Hausheer, Herman, "Duplicities and Integrations of the Personality of St. Augustine: A Study in the Psychology of Genius" (An M.A. Thesis deposited with the Iowa State University Library).

Heisey, Paul Harold, *Psychological Studies in Lutheranism,* Chapter II, "A Study in the Mysticism of Luther" (Burlington, Iowa, The German Literary Board, 1916).

Hirsch, W., *Genius and Degeneration* (New York, D. Appleton & Co., 1896).

Hügel, Baron von, *The Mystical Element of Religion* (New York, Dent & Co., 1909).

Jacobs, Henry Eyster, *Martin Luther* of the series *Heroes of the Reformation,* edited by Samuel Macauley Jackson (New York, G. P. Putnam & Sons, 1907).

James, William *Psychology* in Two Volumes (New York, Henry Holt & Co., 1910). *The Varieties of Religious Experience* (New York, Longmans, Green and Co., 1902).

Jastrow, Morris Jr., *The Study of Religion* (London, Walter Scott, 1901).

Joly, *Psychologie des grands hommes* (1893).

Jones, Ernest, *Papers on Psychoanalysis* (William Wood & Co.).

Jones, R. M., *Studies in Mystical Religion* (London, The Macmillan Co., 1909).

Jung, C. G., *Psychology of the Unconscious* (Moffat, Yard & Co.) *The Psychological Foundation of Belief in Spirits* (Proc. S.P.R., May, 1920).

Kostlin, Julius, *Life of Luther* (translated from the German, 1898).

Lambert, J. F., *Luther's Hymns* (Philadelphia, General Council Publication House, 1917).

Larned, J. W., *A Study of Greatness in Men* (Boston and New York, Houghton Mifflin Co., 1911).

Lauterbach, *Tagebuch.*

Leuba, J. H., "On the Psychology of a Group of Mystics" (*Mind,* Vol. 14., 1905).

Lombroso, Cesare, *The Man of Genius* (London, W. Scott, 1891).

Luther, Martin, The Complete Editions of Luther's Works appearing in German:
    1. Wittenberg   Edition 1539-1559
    2. Jena   Edition 1555-1558

3. Altenburg   Edition 1661-1664
4. Leipsic   Edition 1729-1740
5. Walch   Edition 1740-1753
6. Erlangen   Edition 1826-1857
7. Kaiser or Weimar Edition 1883
8. St. Louis-Walch   Edition 1883

English Editions:

Martin Luther—Precious and Sacred Writings, translated by J. N. Lenker and others—(incomplete).

Works of Martin Luther (joint-editorship) published by the A. J. Holman Co., Philadelphia. (Two Volumes have thus far appeared, 1923.)

Luther on Galatians (Philadelphia, John Highlands, 1891).

Luther's Correspondence and other Contemporary Letters, Vol. I, translated and edited by Preserved Smith. Vol. II by P. Smith and Charles M. Jacobs. Vol. III not yet in press. (Philadelphia, The Lutheran Publication Society, 1913, 1918).

Mathesius, *Tischreden.*

McGiffert, A. C., *Protestant Thought Before Kant* (New York, Scribner's Sons, 1922).

————, *Martin Luther, The Man and His Work* (New York, The Century Co., 1917).

Michelet, *Life of Luther,* collected and arranged, translated by Hazlitt. (London, 1893).

Morris, J. G., *Quaint Sayings and Doings of Martin Luther* (Philadelphia, Lutheran Publication Society).

Nisbet, *Insanity of Genius,* (1891).

Pfister, Oskar, *The Psychoanalytic Method* (Moffat, Yard & Co., 1907).

Pratt, J. B., *The Religious Consciousness* (New York, Macmillan Co., 1920), Chapter III, "Religion and the Subconscious."

Prince, Morton, *The Dissociation of a Personality* (New York, Longmans, Green & Co., 1908).

Reu, J. M., *Thirty-five Years of Luther Research* (Chicago, Wartburg Publishing House, 1917).

Ribot, Th., *Psychology of Emotions* (New York, Scribner's Sons); *Diseases of Personality* (The Open Court Publishing Co.).

Sander, J., *Devotional Readings from Luther's Works for Every Day of the Year* (Rock Island, Illinois, The Augustana Book Concern).

Schlagenhaufen, *Aufzeichnungen.*

Seeburg, Reinhold, *Text-Book Of The History of Doctrines,* translated by Chas. E. Hay (in two volumes), (Philadelphia, The United Lutheran Publication House, 1905).

Sidis, B., *The Psychology of Suggestion* (New York, Appleton, 1911).

Sidis and Goodhart, *Multiple Personality* (New York, Appleton, 1905).

Smith, Preserved, *The Life and Letters of Martin Luther* (Boston, Houghton Mifflin Co., 1911).

———, *Luther's Table-Talk—A Critical Study* (New York, Columbia University Studies, 1907, Vol. XXVI, No. 2).

————, "Luther's Early Development in the Light of Psycho-Analysis" article in *The American Journal of Psychology,* XXIV, 3, p. 360.

See also Luther, Martin, English Editions (in this Bibliography).

Smith, Preserved and Herbert Percival Gallinger, *Conversations With Luther* (Boston, The Pilgrim Press, 1915).

Söderblom, Nathan, *Humor Och Melankoli Och Andra Lutherstudier* (Uppsala, 1919).

Starbuck, E. D., "Double Mindedness," article in Hastings *Encyclopaedea of Religion and Ethics.*

Stratton, G. M., *The Psychology of The Religious Life* (London, G. Allen & Unwin, Ltd., 1911).

Tuke, D. H., "Double Consciousness" article in *Dict. of Psy. Med.,* 1892.

Turk, H., *The Man of Genius* (London, A. & Ch. Black, 1916).

Weise, *Allgemeine Theorie des Genies* (1889).

White, Wm. A., *Mechanisms of Character Formation* (Nervous and Mental Disease Publishing Co.).

Will, Robert, "La Liberte Chretienne", *Etude sur le principe de la piete chez Luther.* (Strasbourg, 1922).